Loud in the House of Myself

W. W. Norton & Company

New York · London

Loud in the House of Myself

MEMOIR OF A STRANGE GIRL

Stacy Pershall

Throughout this memoir, I have changed names and circumstances of all characters other than my immediate family in order to try to protect the privacy of those with whom I have interacted.

For information about permission to reproduce selections from this book, write to Permissions, W. W. Norton & Company, Inc., 500 Fifth Avenue, New York, NY 10110

For information about special discounts for bulk purchases, please contact W. W. Norton Special Sales at specialsales@wwnorton.com or 800-233-4830

Manufacturing by Courier Westford
Book design by Chris Welch
Artwork by Denise de la Cerda
Production manager: Anna Oler

Library of Congress Cataloging-in-Publication Data

Pershall, Stacy.
Loud in the house of myself : memoir of a strange girl / Stacy Pershall. — 1st ed.
p. cm.
ISBN 978-0-393-06692-0 (hardcover)
1. Pershall, Stacy Mental health. 2. Mentally ill—Biography. I. Title.
RC464.P47A3 2011
362.196'890092—dc22
[B]

2010034823

W. W. Norton & Company, Inc.
500 Fifth Avenue, New York, N.Y. 10110
www.wwnorton.com

W. W. Norton & Company Ltd.
Castle House, 75/76 Wells Street, London W1T 3QT

1 2 3 4 5 6 7 8 9 0

For Glenn Becker

Loud in the House of Myself

Prologue

While working at a shop in Brooklyn, my tattoo artist Denise had an apprentice named Tasha. One day we were all hanging out in the shop looking at a book of tattoo designs by the legendary artist Sailor Jerry. The drawings were crude but beautiful, and we laughed at three little pieces that had obviously been some sailors' nicknames years ago. The first one was an eight ball, and beneath it, in plain block letters, it said, "8-ball." The next was a beer keg, and underneath it said, "Guzzler." But the best by far was the third, a crossed fork and knife, with the words "Chow Hound." It didn't take long before Tasha and I decided that, once she had Denise's approval, she'd tattoo "Chow Hound" on my butt. And indeed, one night several months later, Tasha got out her machine and half an hour later I had Chow Hound on my ass. While lying there with the two of them cackling over my flesh, I thought, what in God's name am I doing? Here I am, a former anorexic, getting a tattoo proclaiming that not only do I like to eat, I like to eat a lot.

I am trying on identities again.

It's 1978, and I'm with my mother in the Kmart in Fayetteville, Arkansas, which, at age seven, seems like the big city to me. I sit at a dressing table, wearing a Farrah Fawcett-style wig (because in those days, Kmart sold wigs) and a large floppy beige hat that is supposed to look like straw but is actually made of cheap nylon. Perched precariously on my nose is a pair of pink-tinted sunglasses several sizes too big. I am eating puffy peppermint meringue candies, for which my mother has not yet paid, and writing in a small blue notebook with yellow pages and a cutesy drawing of a flapper on the cover, for which she also has not yet paid. This is important work. I am taking notes.

Two women pass me and giggle. I glance at their reflections in the dressing table mirror and proceed to record every detail of their appearance and conversation, congratulating myself on how inconspicuous I am. I am Harriet the Spy, and I am training myself to be as surreptitious as possible.

Kmart doesn't have everything my mother wants, so we make a stop at Wal-Mart, which, besides the various Baptist churches in the area, is the hub of northwest Arkansas social life. My mother stops to chat with someone she knows and I am free. Wigless now, myself again, I run for my next disguise.

The crafts section is in the far right corner of the store, a distant wonderland of rickrack, fake flowers, and cheap fabric.

In Wal-Mart, I am a dancer. I have the power to defy gravity. I fold myself into the bolts of multicolored mesh, trying to wrap myself so that it completely obscures my vision. I want to see nothing but my future, nothing but the costume I will wear when I am a decade older and famous and thousands of miles away from my thousand-person hometown of Prairie Grove, twenty miles south of Fayetteville. With age will come grace and sophistication. I will be magically teleported to New York City on waves of talent. I will be carried on a magic carpet of tulle. This is what I live for. It is what I have to believe to survive.

I learned about New York City from an episode of *The Love Boat* featuring Andy Warhol. He prowled around the ship with a Polaroid camera, a silver wig, and a pair of big red plastic glasses. From that point on, I relentlessly compared Prairie Grove to New York and knew it was where I belonged.

Prairie Grove is one of those small towns that seem removed from time. Fayetteville is, like the rest of America, being subsumed by subdivisions and strip malls, but Prairie Grove has hardly changed at all. There is still no McDonald's, no Starbucks. There are still only two traffic lights. They still hang the same battered light-up Santas and snowmen they've used for at least thirty years on the light poles of Main Street at Christmas.

You can still stroll past Lou Anna Bellman's flower shop, and if the door is open you'll smell carnations. You can fill prescriptions at Rexall Drug, where the same cracked orange plastic sign still announces the place, and the same three bottles of Lemon-Up shampoo sit on a half-empty shelf, a layer of dust cascading like snow down their plastic lemon caps. There are still cowboy boots and stiff indigo Wrangler's to be bought at Crescent's, where the dressing room still has pine paneling.

At the other end of the street is the Farmers & Merchants Bank and the Beehive Diner, where the air is saturated with countless years of cigarette smoke, cooking grease, and stale coffee, and the same faded photos of chimps in human clothing, dumping plates of spaghetti over their heads, still hang on the wall. The old Laundromat is still there, but the front of it is now a beauty shop.

Once you've ridden your bike through the ditch outside the Dersams' house enough times, and made multiple barefoot treks to the One-Stop Mart to get the same slightly overfrozen Rocky Road ice cream cones, and worn a path through the overgrown field that is a shortcut between Marna Lynn Street and home, you've basically seen it all. If you're a strange and sensitive kid, you're ready to blow the joint by the time you're seven.

And I was that kid, the weird kid, the strange girl, the crazy one. In a town of a thousand people, reputations are hard to live down. There was a forced intimacy there I am deeply grateful not to have today, in New York City, where even though I'm a tattooed lady with flaming red dreadlocks, I can exist in relative anonymity on a day-to-day basis. In Prairie Grove, people thought nothing of going to the gas station barefoot or with perm rods in their hair; they knew their neighbors well enough they might as well have been in their own living room. When you went to town, you saw the same characters, like the old lady who rode around with her poodle in the basket of her bike, or Mary Frances the square-dance teacher, or the unsmiling Hendersons, with their five kids lined up in the driveway half an hour before all the garage sales opened. And, most spectacularly and terrifyingly, there was Susannah, the March of Dimes poster child.

Susannah was the younger sister of Sheridan, one of the most popular girls in school, and she had a disease called Apert syndrome, which meant her face was all messed up, the middle part sunken in and her eyes bulging. They hung her posters in the window of Dillon's grocery store, and although they terrified me, I had an intense urge to steal one. I wanted to do with it what Ramona Quimby did with her Halloween mask, hiding it under the couch cushions so she could sneak peeks at it and scare herself when she chose. I wanted to have Susannah's picture all to myself, knowing that just beneath my butt on the sofa was her crumpled weird eye. I wanted to stare at her face until I could almost see her reaching out to nub my own with her fused-together fingers, their one large nail growing straight across, then safely turn away at the last possible second. Most of all, I wanted to use her image as a tool, a barometer, that would help me test how off things were inside my head. I would know by how long it took before her picture started to look like it was going to come to life—I often thought photographs or inanimate objects might just do so. As a child, my grasp on reality was tenuous, and it only became more so as I got older. (I spent a lot of time staring at my stuffed animals and looking away just before they turned into demons, as I felt certain they would if I stared too long. I felt compelled to do this most nights before falling asleep, perhaps as a way of assuring myself I had some degree of control over my terror.)

When I saw Susannah's mother pushing her around town in her tiny wheelchair, goose bumps swam to the surface of my skin. Anytime I left the house, I took the chance of seeing her, which meant I sometimes wanted to leave the house and sometimes didn't. It depended on how out-of-control my thoughts already were that day. *Make me crippled,* I prayed at night, *make me like Susannah: make it able to be seen. Give me bright shiny crutches with gray plastic cuffs and free me from living in this brain. Make me pretty or hideous but nothing in between. Pose me on matted beige carpet, save me on film, hang me in the window so my birth defects can be seen. Make it bad enough that parents will tell their kids teasing me isn't funny.*

THIS IS THE story of how a strange girl from Prairie Grove discovered she had a multitude of disorders and how she survived. The names of my disorders came later, and start with *b*: borderline, bipolar, bulimic. The only *a* was anorexia. These disorders have a chicken-and-egg quality. Was I bulimic because I was borderline, anorexic before bulimic, is the bipolar even real? Some physicians and researchers suggest that borderline personality disorder should be reclassified as a mood, rather than personality, disorder, and that in fact it may live on the bipolar spectrum. The symptoms overlap. If your mood swings last a week, you're bipolar; if they last a few hours, you're borderline. This is of course a drastic oversimplification, and when you're in the midst of colossal emotional overwhelm, you don't care what your disorder is called, you just want it to stop—or, in the case of early mania, go on forever.

It's only slightly better as an adult. You give your feelings melodramatic names, grandiose status, because melodramatic and grandiose are how you're feeling. You're the most depressed person EVER, or, on the rare good days, the happiest—no, not happy, ECSTATIC. There is no gray, there is only the blackest black and shimmering white. The white, for which you live, is like being illuminated by a god in whom you have long since stopped believing. The black is what you more often get.

If you are this child, or this hypersensitive, emotionally skinless adult who might as well be a child, there will be therapists, long lines of them, each offering drugs and, if you have no health insurance, as much counseling as they can offer before their internships expire. Then it's on to the next one, who may or may not have a different diagnosis and/or different drugs. The drugs usually make you gain weight and sleep a lot—or not at all—but if you're lucky they lift the blackness for a while. If you're bipolar, you tend to only show up in therapists' offices when depressed, which means you will likely be diagnosed with unipolar depression and fed a steady stream of antidepressants, which will send you into glorious hypomania for a while before bottoming out and leaving you desolate again. It will generally take quite some time before someone works with you long enough to see that you have more than just depression, that there is a cycle to your moods.

I was diagnosed in this order: bulimia, major depression, attention deficit disorder (briefly, in 1993, when it first became trendy; it was later discounted), bipolar disorder, anorexia, borderline personality disorder. The first and last diagnoses were most accurate. In the spring of 2005, I entered a three-day-a-week Dialectical Behavioral Therapy (DBT) program for borderlines at NewYork-Presbyterian Hospital. The skills learned in the four modules of DBT—Mindfulness, Distress Tolerance, Emotion Regulation, and Interpersonal Effectiveness—are things most people learn as children. Borderlines, however, due to having been raised in what DBT creator Marsha Linehan calls an "invalidating environment," need help figuring out how not to drown in the undertow of our own feelings.

It is embarrassing to admit I didn't begin to acquire these skills until the age of thirty-four, when after a breakdown I began to get my life together through medication, therapy, and tatooing. *Borderline* means you're one of those girls who walk around wearing long sleeves in the summer because you've carved up your forearms over your boyfriend. You make pathetic suicidal gestures and write bad poetry about them, listen to Ani DiFranco albums on endless repeat, end up in the emergency room for overdoses, scare off boyfriends by insisting they tell you they love you five hundred times a day and hacking into their email to make sure they're not lying, have a police record for shoplifting, and your tooth enamel is eroded from purging. You've had five addresses and eight jobs in three years, your friends are avoiding your phone calls, you're questioning your sexuality, and the credit card companies are after you. It took a lot of years to admit that I was exactly that girl, and that the diagnostic criteria for the disorder were essentially an outline of my life:

[Borderline Personality Disorder is characterized by] a pervasive pattern of instability of interpersonal relationships, self-image, and affect, and marked impulsivity beginning by early adulthood and present in a variety of contexts, as indicated by five (or more) of the following:

1. *Frantic efforts to avoid real or imagined abandonment. Note: Do not include suicidal or self-mutilating behavior covered in criterion 5.*
2. *A pattern of unstable and intense interpersonal relationships characterized by alternating between extremes of idealization and devaluation*
3. *Identity disturbance: markedly and persistently unstable self-image or sense of self*
4. *Impulsivity in at least two areas that are potentially self-damaging (e.g., spending, sex, substance abuse, reckless driving, binge eating). Note: Do not include suicidal or self-mutilating behavior covered in criterion 5.*
5. *Recurrent suicidal behavior, gestures, or threats, or self-mutilating behavior*
6. *Affective instability due to a marked reactivity of mood (e.g., intense episodic dysphoria, irritability, or anxiety usually lasting a few hours and only rarely more than a few days)*
7. *Chronic feelings of emptiness*
8. *Inappropriate, intense anger or difficulty controlling anger (e.g., frequent displays of temper, constant anger, recurrent physical fights)*
9. *Transient, stress-related paranoid ideation or severe dissociative symptoms*

The first time I read these criteria, I felt like someone had been following me around taking notes. DBT and tattoos taught me how to accept and survive pain, a lesson I needed to learn physically as well as emotionally. Tattooing, like therapy, has allowed me to control the occasions on and degree to which I experience discomfort. I would not go back to my life before age thirty-five for anything in the world, but life after is shaping up to be pretty good.

Throughout my life I've felt the constant pull between a powerful force that wants to make art and save the world and one that wants to destroy me and everyone in my path. I have been driven by a frantic need for overachievement, which becomes even more frantic when I'm hypomanic. My mood goes up, I commit myself to grandiose plans, I feel certain I can take on the universe. In my case, for every seventy-two hours of unadulterated manic bliss, there are weeks of unremitting depression and obsessive rumination. These are the psychiatric cards I was dealt. I have lost years to depression so crippling I lay in bed for days at a time, my head sunken into my pillow because I couldn't bear its weight.

But this body in which I am trapped is made, now, of color and life. My skin is made of lightning bolts, robots, rockets, cats, the Bride of Frankenstein, Laurie Anderson quotes. My tattoos remind me who I am and what I'm made of, and the unfilled lines of a work in progress remind me where I want to go. Learning who I am and creating a skin in which I can bear to live has taken this long and required this much effort.

Let's go back to Prairie Grove, 1978, the beginning, and you'll see why.

1

THE FIRST TATTOO *I ever saw was on my uncle's middle finger. It was the number* 13, *because he'd done it himself on his* thir-teen *birthday.*

"*It doesn't really look like a* 13," *I said.* "*It kind of looks like a lowercase* b."

"*Yeah, the top half of the* 3 *wore off.*"

"*Why?*"

"*Because I didn't know what I was doing.*"

"*Why?*"

"*Because I was thirteen. I was young and stupid.*"

I was seven. Thirteen seemed very old to me. "*I would think a thirteen-year-old would have better penmanship,*" *I said.*

———

11

In first grade, I won a dead frozen rabbit at school for making up the best poem for my teacher's husband's frozen foods
packing company, Pel-Freez, up on Zero Mountain, where
everybody says the Satan worshipers are supposed to be. My
dad says there are no Satan worshipers, there's just a cold-
storage facility built into the side of the Ozark Mountains.
Trucks can drive into the side of this mountain, he says, and
he would know, because he drives a semi for the Willis Shaw
Trucking Company and has to pick up freight there sometimes. When I think of my father's boss, I have an image of a
man who looks like a combination of *Diff'rent Strokes'* Willis
and Snow Miser from the Rankin-Bass *The Year Without a
Santa Claus.* He's there on Zero Mountain telling the trucks
where to take the rabbits.

I won the contest like I win all the others: I can draw. The
day Mrs. Clark asked us to come up with a slogan, I took a
big piece of manila paper and wrote *Get into the Rabbit Habit*
across the top. Then I drew a picture of a blue rabbit's foot, like
the one my dad bought me at a truck stop, on a plate with a
fork beside it. Mrs. Clark's husband liked that I knew how to
rhyme and I knew what "habit" meant. And so on this fateful
night after the contest, as my mother peeled small pink strips
of rabbit out of a blue plastic wrapper and arranged them carefully in a frying pan, I sat smug, proud to have provided for
my family.

We had moved into our new house on Linda Street only
a few weeks before. Prior to that we lived in a drafty rental
house with hardwood floors that froze your feet in the morning, and pink and black tiles on the bathroom wall my mom

said disdainfully were left over from the 1950s, but now we had our own place with brand-new rust-colored carpet and slick wood paneling on the walls. After we ate the rabbit, I snuggled against my mother's pregnant belly on our new brown-and-orange plaid couch, listening to my brother beneath her skin, smelling the plastic-scented velour and the chemical loveliness of the new carpet, until the pool salesman came.

In Arkansas in the 1970s, people came to your house to try to sell you stuff and you actually let them in. You offered them a cup of coffee, listened to their speech, and then, if they were lucky, purchased from them a piece of the American Dream. I found the pool salesman more captivating than the man who sold us encyclopedias the week before. The pool man had his own little TV, a beige box on which he played movies of different pools he could construct in our backyard. They were made of seafoam-green aluminum, with plastic liners in the same shade of blue as the Howard Johnson's logo or the word "mart" in Kmart, that turquoise that went so well with orange. I was fascinated by a close-up of the pool's built-in skimmer, a little box that sucked the dead bugs out of the water. I gnawed at a snack-size Baby Ruth, my seventh, and nobody noticed; my parents too were transfixed by the clacking skimmer disposing of shiny black beetles and dragonflies with disintegrating wings. I shoved the Baby Ruth wrappers back into the bag after I ate each one so that, if my mom happened to look my way, it would appear I was still on my first. My stomach began to churn a bit, the candy bars mixing with the rabbit in an unpleasant manner, but I kept eating because I could.

The salesman did his job; my parents bought a pool that night. They were determined to provide me and my forthcoming brother, Cameron, with all the trappings of a standard suburban childhood—*World Book* encyclopedias, aboveground pools, new bikes from Sears, Swanson chicken dinners with stray corn kernels baked into the brownies served on avocado-green-and-gold TV trays, and individually wrapped Halloween candy bars any time of the year. With our new one-story yellow house came a yard with a chain-link fence, a real driveway instead of gravel, and a garage instead of a carport. When the concrete driveway was poured, my dad wrote "Butch, Karen, Stacy, 1977" in it with a stick. When the pool man got up to leave, I opened my mouth to ask him if he wanted to see it, but I threw up instead.

My mother said, "Oh no!" and she picked me up in both arms and dashed into the bathroom, where we didn't even make it to our new toilet with the Eljer sticker still on the side before I threw up again. She lay me on the counter in my wet pajamas and held my pigtails back while I retched into the sink. A decade later I would puke into the toilet every day, picking at the faded Eljer sticker with my fingernails, and pray my mother wouldn't find me. Every time I'd remember the night we ate the rabbit and bought the pool, in which I would do hours of water aerobics, and I'd still want my mother to hold me. I would remember how she rested one hand between my shoulders and with her other hand held my golden hair. All the force of my small body heaving couldn't shake her loose.

———

MY MOTHER WASN'T a debutante, and she wasn't a sorority girl. She was like most other girls from the Prairie Grove High School Class of '68: she married at eighteen and gave birth to me at twenty, and until she was twenty-six I was her life. We weren't poor, but we certainly weren't rich; we lived on a truck driver's salary. In Prairie Grove driving trucks is a good job, and it is an especially good job if you're doing it for Wal-Mart. But in the seventies, if you couldn't drive for Wal-Mart, it was a decent gig to drive for Willis Shaw, so we always had food on the table. Even before we moved into the yellow house, I had plastic toys and homemade sandboxes and plastic kiddie pools that faded and cracked and lasted only a season. I had tuna fish sandwiches on toast and Nacho Cheese Doritos and red Kool-Aid, which I consumed while watching Fat Albert on Saturdays at noon. I had fake babies with too many accessories, fake bottles with fake orange juice that disappeared when you upended the hard plastic nipple between the doll's immobile lips. I had these things to teach me what to be, and still I didn't get it right. I was never very good at being girly.

My mother claims she didn't know how strange I was until she had Cameron, someone to whom she could compare me. Before he was born, she thought it was normal, in fact delightful, when I asked her to light a candle to set atop my toy piano and refused to speak to her unless she addressed me as Schroeder. "Say cheese, Schroeder," she'd laugh, and snap a square picture of me with her little black camera. When I cut a hole in the bottom of a plastic Halloween pumpkin and set it over my head, she simply said, "Come to dinner, Headless

Horseman." She read my shorthand, spoke my language. That
is, of course, until she didn't.

My daddy was my hero, a spinner of yarns, a bringer-home
of the world. I close my eyes now and conjure my earliest memories of him: he reenters our lives a few times a month, a gust
of cold behind him, that icicled Arkansas winter that somehow
still smells like cut grass, and he's wearing a green corduroy
coat with a big brown furry collar, and he picks me up and
hugs me. He smells like Mennen Skin Bracer aftershave and
diesel fuel, and his big sideburns scratch my face. He has one
silver tooth and three other fake ones he can take out, and
sometimes he even lets me hold them. He calls it a "bridge,"
and it hooks onto his real teeth with pointy silver tendrils. He
always has a present for me when he comes in off the road. The
piñata was a big one, but even the smaller ones are mesmeriz-
ing: Icee Critters, the little plastic animals they hang on your
cup at Sonic, or a monkey with cymbals who screeches when
you smack him on the head, or a run of blow-up animals. He
tells me these things came from truck stops, and I imagine
that truck stops must be the most magical places on earth.
I save the Icee Critters in a Folger's coffee can, which I bury
just outside the back door and dig up frequently to reacquaint
myself with my treasure. I use the monkey with cymbals as a
metronome while I practice at our avocado-green piano. And
in the background, in the doorway to the kitchen, my mother
stands and watches, knowing that I will eventually leave her
too, and that she will need another baby to take my place.

My father was the fifth of eight children, the first by minutes of twins. His mother, my grandmother, Katie Lee Pershall,

had already decided on Cheryl as a girl's name, so my father became Jeryl, for obvious reasons. He had brothers named Royce and Weldon and sisters named Joy Nell and Eva Gay, so it could be argued that he made out better than he could have. But Weldon proclaimed that he would call no brother of his such a sissy name as Jeryl, and from that point on my dad was known as Butch.

When he was seventeen, my father spent months planning to move to Los Angeles with six friends to seek his fortune. But when moving day came and my dad rolled up in his packed '57 Chevy, ready to go, his friends laughed at him and said they were just joking around. My father, righteous with the anger that drives Pershalls to destruction, drove to California alone, just to prove a point. He got himself a room and a job as a fork-lift driver at a door factory. After a year, homesickness drove him back to the Ozarks. Home again, he joined the National Guard, got his GED, and started driving for Willis Shaw. My dad's best friend, my soon-to-be-uncle, John "Junior" Kelley— he of the *13* on his finger—was at that time dating my mom's older sister Linda. It wasn't long before my parents got fixed up on their first double date. They went fishing on a July after-noon at Bud Kidd Lake with Junior and Linda, and two Julys later, in 1968, they married. My mother wore a white mini-dress and a bouffant June Carter hairdo; my dad, porkchop sideburns, a flattop, and a black suit with a skinny tie. It is after he lost his teeth but before he got the bridge, so there is a hole in his excited, terrified smile. In their wedding photos, they look painfully young and blissfully unaware, stunned by the flash cubes on several Instamatic cameras at once. They do not yet know about things like crazy daughters who make themselves throw up.

Shortly after they married, my parents settled in Prairie Grove in the rental house, owned by a couple named George and Ethel, who lived next door in a massive, funky Victorian that was always one paint job away from beautiful. My mother, armed with her new high school diploma, got a job at the Baldwin Piano factory. She worked there for two years, making piano keys, until she found out she was pregnant with me. It was an uneventful pregnancy. But I was born yellow, jaundiced, and they had to put me in an incubator with patches over my eyes. My mother cried the day she left me at the hospital while the other mothers took their babies home. Twice a day for a week she made the half-hour drive to the hospital to feed me, until finally they pronounced me pink enough to leave, and my father drove us both home in the massive white Buick, a car too big to be contained by a garage.

ONE EVENING DURING my sixth summer, when the dogwoods were abloom with white petals, my mother and I walked home from Ethel's house carrying a jar of homemade plum jam and a bag of freshly cut spearmint.

"Mommy," I said, "is Ethel your friend?"

"I guess so," she said.

"Have you ever gone to the movies with her?" For some reason I thought this was what adults did with their friends— they went to the movies.

She laughed. "No, I've never gone to the movies with her."

"Who's your best friend?"

"Linda, I guess," she said,

"But she's your sister." I didn't think sisters or aunts or cousins counted.

"Well then," she said, "I guess Grandma."

The fact that my mother had no friends became a matter of increasing concern to me. I didn't like that she didn't go to the movies. I felt sorry for her and didn't want to leave her side. When she was with me, I did whatever I could to make sure she was having fun, and I took this upon myself with a resolute determination. I could not bear to see my mother sad.

I hid my dolls from her. Not because they were girly and I preferred Hot Wheels cars (which I did) or because they were creepy (which they were), but because I could picture my mother holding one of them and sobbing if I was dead. If I died, she would have no one. She would have to play with a doll and pretend it was a baby, like the old lady we saw at the nursing home when my Brownie troop went there to sing Christmas carols.

I lay awake at night imagining my own death, and what came afterward. In Sunday school they told us Christians lived forever in heaven, but this offered me no comfort. I never worried about what I would do if my mother died, only what she would do if I died. She would be sad, and the last thing I would see before I went to heaven would be her sad face. She might be crying. She might already be holding the doll.

When she told me she was going to have another baby, I felt a profound sense of relief. There would be someone else to split the job of entertaining her. Before her pregnancy, when my dad was on the truck, which was most of the time, I was all she had. I played the piano for her a lot, but sometimes I got tired. I made up plays and dances and songs for her. I wrote her books, stories written and illustrated in blue ballpoint pen on pink stenographer's paper, bound with my Snoopy stapler. I made her sno-cones with my Snoopy Sno-Cone Machine, and when I took ceramics classes at Ethel's craft shop, everything I made was for her. Our cabinets were packed with my meticulously painted plaster witches and Santas and Easter bunnies; I thoroughly equipped her for all seasonal contingencies. In her room were ceramic jewelry boxes, in the kitchen a ceramic cowbell shaped like an actual cow. I never made anything for myself, but for my mother I made elaborate plastic jewelry and latch-hook rugs and loop 'n' loom potholders. I saved my allowance to buy her things from the Avon catalog; her bathroom counter was littered with glass owls filled with solid perfume.

Because I needed someone else to help me, another set of hands on the assembly line, I couldn't wait for the baby to come. We talked about names. One late-summer night, while she scrubbed my back in our pink bathtub, she told me I could pick the middle name if the baby was a girl. I tried to choose between Jane and Nancy. She said the first name would be Natalie, so Jane was better. Unlike many children who are jealous when a sibling comes along, I loved sharing my mother with the person growing in her belly. The world was full of possibilities. My sister. White petals fell from the dogwoods outside our expectant home.

Natalie Jane died on Christmas. She was never born; she died while she was still inside my mother's womb. While we were opening our presents, my mother started bleeding. The next day my dad took me to see her in the hospital. I made her a green construction-paper tree with cotton balls glued on for snow, and she fed me lemon Jell-O from her avocado-green dinner tray. I tried not to think about the fact that my sister had, according to my father, "something too wrong with her to be born." I tried not to imagine what her face might have looked like.

When my mother came home, she stared out the kitchen window and cried a lot. She still took me places and did things with me, but a part of her was gone. I tried hard to be very good and entertaining so she wouldn't miss Natalie Jane. So that I wouldn't bother her or see her cry, I hid in my room, picking out fantasy mothers from the JCPenney catalog. I spent hours naming the people on every page: first name, last name, middle name sometimes too. Then I faked their signatures, because that made them seem more real, more like people I actually knew. The arrival of the Penney's catalog each Christmas may have excited other kids because they couldn't wait to start making lists of the things they wanted, but it excited me because there were more people to name, more mothers and sisters to make up. I created entire JCPenney families, sometimes folding back the pages of women's wear to touch children's wear so I could assign smiling besweatered mothers to offspring in cozy quilted pajamas. I asked my grandma if I could have her catalogs when she was done with them; that way, I could name the same people all over again. I became obsessed with classification, as if by making enough lists and putting everything in exactly the right order and calling everything by exactly the right name, I could save both my mother and myself. I began "collecting friends" when we went shopping: in the mall, I walked up to random women with a pen and a paper bag from the Hallmark store. If they agreed to be my friends, I asked them to sign their names on the bag. I kept the bag under my mattress, pulling it out and meticulously copying the signatures next to my JCPenney mothers.

My mom told me she was pregnant again a year later. I prayed she would carry this baby all the way, and—I was convinced this was due solely to my asking Jesus enough times—she did. My brother Cameron Jeryl came into the world on a cold March day in 1978, a few months after we moved into our new yellow house. My father picked me up from school, telling me there was someone at the house who wanted to meet me, and that day I held a baby for the first time. He had thick black hair and small pursed lips, and his milky blue eyes were closed like a kitten's. I loved him instantly, and liked to set his carrier next to me on the piano bench while I played. I told him the names of the songs. I explained to him why Bach was better than Mozart (the fingering was harder) and why Beethoven was better than both of them (he was deaf but still wrote music). Cameron slept and gurgled and eventually cried, and my mother swept him into her arms like she used to do with me.

Now that my mother had a baby, she was hypervigilant about his safety. Once, after he'd started to climb, he pulled himself up on a chair, then lost his balance; the chair tipped over and he fell to the floor. My mother's back had been turned, and now Cameron had a concussion. I'm not sure she ever forgave herself. She began to slip away into an obsession with protecting him. When he got sick two months later and ended up in the hospital with a high fever and aching joints, she spent every minute with him while I stayed with Aunt Linda and my cousins Kendra and Jason. I rattled about in their big house, twice the size of ours, wondering if I would ever see my mom or my brother again.

One night, I heard the unmistakable sound of my mother crying in Linda's living room. I crept out of bed and sat on the landing above the stairs, twisting the multicolored shag carpet in my fingers, straining to hear the conversation downstairs. I heard my mother say Cameron had to have a spinal tap. They thought he had meningitis. I imagined a tap like the one I'd read about in *Little House on the Prairie*, the kind Pa stuck into trees to get the maple syrup that Laura and Mary froze in the snow to make candy. Were they going to drain my brother's spine? What kind of syrup was inside a spine?

My mother said, "They told me it would hurt him a lot."

Linda said, "But it's the only way they can find out what's wrong."

My mother said, "I know," and cried.

I lay on my side, buried one ear in the carpet, and covered the other one with my hand. I started tapping my foot. It calmed me to count the taps. I fell asleep there, wishing my mother would come and tell me she remembered me. I thought of the rabbit and how she'd once held my hair. I wished I were sick so I could have her back.

Cameron came home from the hospital a week later, healthy as ever. He didn't have meningitis. He looked the same as he had before he left, but my mother looked different. Her face was pale and she wasn't smiling. That night my dad told me he was moving me to the bedroom down the hall and putting Cameron in the room across the hall from his and my mother's. They could hear him better that way.

This is how my mother came to belong profoundly and definitively to my brother. Many years later my dad would tell me she did the same thing to him when I was born—she stopped being his and started being mine. For some reason, she could only belong to one of us at a time.

I watched as she attended with obsessive devotion to Cameron's health. He turned three years old, then four. My mother continued to treat him delicately and fearfully, as if his life depended on her every decision. He parlayed her sympathy into a diet of frozen pizza (meaning he ate it uncooked) and chicken nuggets (cooked), eating almost nothing but these two items for the next several years. He crunched the ice off his pepperoni and my mother hovered over him making sure pieces of frozen meat didn't get stuck in his throat.

I grew separate from my family. At ten years old I went somewhere else. I started to focus on how I looked through the eyes of others, as if their critical gazes could help me fine-tune my image and one day be recognized by my mother for all my talents, intelligence, and compassion. I wanted her love, but I convinced myself I didn't need it. I spent most of my time ensconced in one of the many fantasy worlds I created— Hospital, Mad Science Lab, and a reality I called "Baroney," in which I was an orphan girl who wore a square-dance can-can and lived among the weeds and wildflowers in the empty field behind our house. In Hospital, I lay on my dad's work-bench in the garage reenacting the latest disease-of-the-week movie—the bench was my deathbed and I had cystic fibrosis, or multiple sclerosis, or muscular dystrophy. I flipped through my identities like a card catalog, selecting the one that fit that day, that hour, that minute. I learned how to disappear. This is how it started.

2

THE FIRST TATTOO *I got was for the first girl I loved. She had blue glitter eyes and I loved the way her skull felt through her face. In her room in the summer of 1994 we kicked aside the chicken-wire armatures for her papier-mâché sculptures and fell giggling into bed, whacking our heads against her ballet barre on the way down. She smoked Marlboros while she did pliés to the guitar practice of her ever-changing roommates. She pierced her own nipple in the mirror, and, with things thus put into perspective, I got a tattoo. It was that simple: something needed to be commemorated, marked. I had to do something so permanent I would no longer be allowed to break my promises. It all started with a tiny woman symbol, black, about an inch tall.*

It wasn't just family life that made me retreat. It was also school. If you are an intelligent, overly sensitive, arguably mentally ill child, and you are bullied, you get sicker. Because I preferred reading to recess and drawing to sports, because I made the mistake of telling someone I was going home after school one day to play Mad Science (and that I had a special pair of Inventing Pants with Inventing Suspenders I wore to do so), the popular girls at my school relentlessly teased me. Although I now look at old photographs of myself and see a cute little blond girl, not disfigured or hideous in any way, I believed by age eleven that I was horribly ugly and undeserving of human companionship. I will never understand why schoolgirls need to choose one among them to be the outcast, but that was the role I was given, and it was so excruciating that I broke a cardinal preteen taboo and cried and let them see me cry, often in class. I couldn't keep my emotions inside.

At night I lay in bed unable to sleep, and thoughts of the day's torment filled me up like thick black honey. They stuck to my innards and my brain, they gagged me. The only way to combat them was with the secret rituals I developed. I rubbed my toes frantically in figure eights on my sheets, flexing and releasing my calf muscles in time, and chanted in a whisper to calm the pounding and howling.

My brain turned against me. I felt so undeserving of companionship that if I found ways to soothe myself, I needed an imaginary enemy to dole out an equal and opposite punishment. For some reason, the real enemies weren't enough. I had to be even meaner to myself than they were—the old "nobody can hurt me as much as I can hurt myself." This is how the Bad Dog came to live inside me.

It spent a decade forming, gaining power. It made me fly into rages and cry hysterically at school. It ran through the threads of my nervous system. I was contaminated by it. Girls were not supposed to get as angry as I did.

My fear of the Bad Dog, as well as my terror of being bullied, led me to invent as many excuses as I could to miss school. I wrapped myself up like a burrito in Downy-scented sheets on the couch and settled in for a day of game show reruns and ginger ale. The Bad Dog receded on those days, but I didn't trust the respite: I knew it would come back, because it always did. It would make me do things I didn't want to do, and then I'd have to punish myself. The punishments involved things like sitting outside in my dog's little red plywood house or drinking from a bowl on my hands and knees. It was terribly degrading, but if I degraded myself, then I could soothe myself again. After I performed my penance, I would sit and stroke my hair, pretending I was secretly petting her ears. She and I were in this together. I whispered comforting things to her, like *I kind of want to take care of you.*

One day, back at school after another of my many absences, I sat at my desk trying to concentrate on geography rather than the notes Kyra and Jessica were passing behind me. I heard them whisper "Paranoid Mouse" and giggle. I had stupidly said something in class one day about being afraid of mice, and Jessica, who lived on a farm, gleefully began bringing dead mice to school, securing her acceptance into the popular clique by tormenting me with them. She chased me around the playground with a dead mouse one day, flinging it into the weeds when it looked like the teacher on duty was catching on, running off squealing the gleeful squeals of the newly accepted bully. When I begged to know what I had done and why they were being mean, they said, "We don't hate you. You're just paranoid." If I started crying in class, one of the popular girls would inevitably whisper, "Paranoid Mouse," and I would plug my ears and cry harder.

That afternoon, I found a dead mouse in my lunch box. Torturing me was currency; I began to think my only worth was as a catalyst by which others could become popular. Letting the teachers see the mouse would have made things even worse, so when the bell rang for after-lunch recess, I quickly dumped my food and the stiff mouse into the trash and ran at breakneck speed to the farthest corner of the playground. I wanted to get a head start, to get as far away from the popular girls as I could. I sat on the grass and watched for them, but they never came outside.

Where were they? What were they doing? What were they plotting? I ran back to the building, made some excuse to the teacher guarding the doors about needing to see the nurse, and tiptoed down the empty hall.

I heard them singing.

Their voices came from Mrs. Dunlap's room and sucked me down the hallway. Everyone knew Mrs. Dunlap was the fifth-grade teacher of choice, seeing as how her daughter Sheila had just made the junior high cheerleading team and was thus at the top of the Prairie Grove social hierarchy. Anything you were able to do to gain Mrs. Dunlap's attention made you spe-

cial, made the other girls envious of you. It meant you might
be a cheerleader when you grew up.

I knew as I touched the door handle of the classroom that
I was about to do something embarrassing and wrong, but
the Bad Dog was in charge. *You'll need me,* it said. *I gotcha
covered.*

I opened the door.

The singing stopped when I walked in. They all turned and
stared at me, Bonne-Bell-Orange-Crush-glossed mouths hanging open, looking at me with the same horror and excitement
they'd exhibit if I had just walked into the room naked. I stood
there frozen, hyperaware of my scruffiness, my shirt untucked
and one ponytail higher than the other. The Bad Dog turned
me in on myself like a vortex, gleefully saying, *Look, look.
There they are, here you are. Separate. You do not belong.*

"Stacy," said Kyra, "we're practicing."

"For what?" I creaked, mouth dry, their eyes on my skin.

"For Parents' Night. Mrs. Dunlap picked us yesterday when
you were absent." Behind her, Jessica snickered. Mrs. Dunlap
clapped her hands to bring them back to order, and they all
began singing again, their backs to me, oblivious to my presence, blocking me out. Their hair gleamed in the sun. Their
polo shirts were a field of unsoiled pastel.

I tried to speak but couldn't. I was wailing—or, rather, the
Bad Dog was wailing. Ten minutes later, back in class, I tried
to hide my reddened face behind my science book, but tears
fell onto the pages.

That night, I crept out to the backyard and crawled into
the doghouse with a loaf of Wonder Bread I'd stolen from the

kitchen. It was late spring and the back door was open, the kitchen light casting the checkered shadow of the screen door across the patio. I could see my brother sitting at the table, waiting for my mom to serve him his frozen pizza.

I thought that perhaps if I could cram myself into a small enough space, my brain would also be contained. Often, when I came home from school in the afternoons, I would drag my quilt from the bed to the closet, spread it over my shoes, and tuck myself into it in a fetal position. I felt I deserved to be poked by shoes and toys and whatever else I'd shoved in there by way of cleaning my room. In the middle of the night, terror-stricken by recurrent nightmares, I folded my quilt around me and went flying down the hall toward my parents' room, bat wings of blanket billowing behind me, and crawled as stealthily as possible into the foot of space between their bed and the wall. Although I woke up with a stiff neck and tingling limbs, I slept better there than I ever did in my own bed. My father's snores soothed me.

There were no shrinks in Prairie Grove, but there was a church on every corner, with their oft-misspelled signs out front promising happiness and salvation. Like every other kid I knew, I had logged my share of hours in Sunday school, making Bibles out of bars of Ivory soap wrapped in a black velvet cover cut with pinking shears, the crosses on the front made of sequins and straight pins. My mother had several vases made of A.1. steak sauce bottles covered with masking tape and brown shoe polish, a popular church crafts activity, though I was never quite sure what those had to do with Jesus. I had even once gotten, as a prize for memorizing the most New Tes-

tament verses, to take home the class mascot, a weird cardboard puppet named Mr. Bible Beaver. I liked singing in the
Christmas pageants and going to the various Vacation Bible
Schools every summer (in which the Baptist, Methodist, and
Presbyterian churches all had the same watery Kool-Aid and
Hydrox cookies instead of Oreos). But that year I became a true
religious fanatic. While other kids were out riding their bikes
and playing, I was in my bedroom watching *The 700 Club* and
praying for people's livers. Although I suspected there were
better things for mentally disturbed thirteen-year-old girls to
do than log so many hours kneeling in prayer that they got
rugburn, for the first time my brain was filled with something
other than my own misery. Fervent prayer was perfect for me;
I already loved repetition and chants. I was more than happy
to pray for the innards of strangers in Iowa.

My childhood was a time in which a slow and thorough
plow went trawling through my heart, digging irrevocable
trenches. I filled them the only way I knew how: with Jesus.

3

WHEN HANNAH AITCHISON *tattooed Eve (of Garden of Eden fame) from my left ribs down to my hip bone, I felt somewhat blasphemous, like I was doing something I had been warned a long time ago would send me to hell. After all, she's naked, though her naughty bits are covered by the snake that twists around her, holding an apple in its mouth. I've blocked a lot of the Bible from my brain, because for so long it was used primarily to scare me. But Eve was a woman who wanted what she shouldn't, and for that reason, she has always been my favorite character in the Bible. Eve took chances. She was the first woman to buck the system, to realize that beauty carries risk but is worth it nonetheless. As the story goes, Eve was responsible for the whole of human suffering, but without her sacrifice, I wouldn't know the flavor of*

pink cotton candy, wouldn't know my cat smells like melted snow,
wouldn't have started getting tattooed. Because what is a tattoo,
really, but suffering that brings with it beauty?

I remember the night of my first barbecue with the Baptist
church's youth group as Act One of a protracted sexual awak-
ening that took place during the summer and fall of 1984. I
was invited to the cookout by a geeky boy named Brian, the
type who plays in the band and would be a Dungeons & Drag-
ons freak if it weren't a sin against Jesus. Although I considered myself a devout servant of Christ, I was still somehow
able to overlook the fact that lusting after a married man was
a sin, and became possessed by a fervent desire to fuck my
youth group leader.

His name was Michael, and he was a cross between Max
Headroom and Adonis. He had hulking muscles and hulking
teeth, and he was playing volleyball when I first laid eyes on
him. The whole scene is, of course, speckled in my mind with
flakes of sunlit Coppertone gold, like the bright pops at the
end of a Super 8 movie. I actually remember thinking, *My
loins are aflame,* a phrase I had read or heard somewhere that
seemed appropriate in the moment. I thanked Jesus. I prayed
for two things: the will to starve, and Michael's love.

By this point I had become the quintessential unpopular
adolescent. Although I wasn't quite as much of an outcast as
the kids who didn't bathe or the ones who had already started
to smoke, I was still a compulsive reader and I sucked at sports.
Therefore, even if I hadn't had premature acne, my popularity still would have had a ceiling. As far as religion itself, I

had never known anything outside of fundamentalist Christianity. Freedom of worship in Prairie Grove meant a choice between First Baptist, First Methodist, First Presbyterian, and the Church of Christ. Each church had its own reputation: the old people went to Methodist, the rednecks went to Presbyterian, and the Holy Rollers went to the Church of Christ, where they spoke in tongues and the girls couldn't cut their hair or wear pants (meaning that as soon as they got to school, they changed into the tight, slutty jeans they had hidden in their lockers and headed straight for the bathroom to trowel on their makeup). The First Baptist church had a reputation as having the most active youth group, Ultimate Frisbee tournaments, and weekly cookouts—all of which appealed to me.

At the barbecue where I fell for Michael we ate hamburgers, played volleyball, and then went into the dimly lit air-conditioned church to watch a film about rock 'n' roll records and how they were tools of the devil. Christian teenagers were shown gleefully flinging albums onto a fire in a trash can, and as the albums began to pile up, the camera began to zoom in, until the entire screen was filled with melting albums and flames. Some of the albums, said the voice-over, even *screamed*, they were so packed with evil. Then a picture of Satan's face faded in from the background. The narrator talked about all the secular means by which teens could be led astray from Christ, with music being, apparently, one of the devil's favorite weapons. The bad production values and garish film stock made me feel kind of sick to my stomach, so I watched Michael instead. He was about twenty-five, and he was married. His blond wife Pauline sat next to him, and when they bowed their heads to pray, she stroked his back gently, lovingly, and I imagined both her arms around him, and they were making out, naked, and *ohhh* . . .

I started going to church all the time. I tried to dress sexy when I went, or like a wholesome Christian version of sexy. I never got it quite right. I had already made some early stabs at New Wave clothing purchases, so I'd walk in wearing a black-and-white-striped miniskirt and pink leggings with dress shoes and a bow in my hair. But because I had tried to cut my hair like Cyndi Lauper, shaving one side and perming the other, it meant that for several months my head looked like an unfortunate prom dress. Still, I continued my zealous march through the doors of the Baptist church on a weekly basis, clutching my New International Version Student Bible and trying to win Michael's favor. I just adored him. I thought it was so cute when he said, "Jammin' for Jesus," his frequent expression of enthusiasm for every situation from revival to a volleyball goal.

He said it after baptizing me in the human-size fish tank above the pulpit. My body, wrapped in a drenched white robe, was visible to the entire congregation through the Plexiglas window of the baptistery. Before Michael baptized me that night, I prayed hard for salvation from myself, begging Jesus to make me someone other, someone better, than I was. I wanted to be Pauline with her mascaraed eyelashes, her slightly overlapping front teeth, her scent of Pantene. I wanted her to crawl into the tank with me and scrub me clean with Procter & Gamble products, harsh abrasives, whatever would take away the invisible sin of the Bad Dog that made my mother ignore me and made my father fly into rages. I wanted to carry the sins of my family, the things we couldn't talk about in public, into that fake rectangular sea and pay for them with my breath and my blood and my heart. I stared through the water at the warbly wood paneling above me, knowing I could come up whenever I wanted, but in making extra sure I'd atoned, I drew out my time underwater just a moment too long. Michael's strong hands suddenly clenched my arms and brought me up for air.

Even after my baptism, I knew there was still something wrong with my head, but I trusted in God to fix it. I made regular trips to Michael's office to confess my mundane junior high sins. I admitted that I sometimes cheated on tests and made my parents mad at me and that most people hated me but I didn't know why.

He said, "It sounds like you feel you don't fit in very well."

I said, "That's right, I don't."

"There are a lot of pressures at school when you're different," said Michael.

I stared at his teeth.

"Christ was different too," he continued. "But now that you've joined the church, you have your brothers and sisters in Jesus to help you walk with Him."

"I've been thinking about giving you my records," I said, surprising myself. "I think maybe part of the reason I'm so sad sometimes is that I'm receiving those messages from Satan. Like in the backwards masking and stuff. Where they tell you to worship the devil."

Michael nodded solemnly.

"So, yeah. I thought that maybe if I gave my records to you, just to keep for a little while, that maybe I could find some, uh, more strength in Christ."

"Let's pray about it," Michael said, taking my hands. Four hundred billion volts shot through me.

The next Sunday, after church, I went to his office and pulled my records from my backpack. I had squeezed my eyes shut, gone on my knees in the dark, and prayed about this offering. I had held my breath and listened for Jesus to talk to me until I was almost sure I heard Him. I relished the chance to tell Michael how Jesus had said to me, *Yes, the Go-Gos are secular, and if you turn over that copy of "We Got the Beat," you and I can speed up a little in our walk.* It pained me to give away my music, as it was the one thing prior to Jesus that had sometimes calmed me. I chose it largely for the rhythms of the lyrics, often replaying one segment of a song over and over again like a chant to soothe me. But I couldn't back out now, and nothing seemed as important as the possibility that Michael might touch me again.

I leaned toward him, there, in his office, where icicles cracked inside the air conditioner and the indoor-outdoor carpet smelled of mold, and I said, "I feel like I'm really beginning to *understand*."

"Jammin'," he said. And he was so sincere, and his teeth were so white, and I closed my eyes and imagined that there were scratches on his back from last night with Pauline, and for one one-zillionth of a second I thought he might kiss me.

But he didn't.

When I found out that church camp was coming up, I

begged my mother to let me go. Thrilled at the prospect of my having any friends at all, even if said friends spent all their time jammin' for the Messiah, she gave me the registration fee and money for snacks, and mined a pair of flowery twin-size sheets from the depths of the bathroom closet for my bunk bed. I couldn't have been more thrilled: I was going to spend a week with Michael in a town called Bogg Springs, a place I imagined would be something of a Christian honeymoon resort.

Of course, as in most things, I was profoundly wrong. I arrived to find that the cabins were made of damp dark wood, with cracked concrete floors and only one window apiece. The bunk beds had microscopically thin, lumpy mattresses. I decided it would be an adventure sleeping up high in the air; I had never slept in a bunk bed. But I was assigned a bottom bunk beneath Darlene, one of the more pious Baptist girls, who wouldn't wear the jeans that were so popular that year, the ones with the flat triangular yoke in front, because they pointed to your crotch and made boys think of sex. To my left was Pauline, Wife of Michael, and I couldn't wait to watch her sleep at night and pretend I was Michael beside her. I could play the twisted, transubstantiationalist spy game at which I was already becoming adept, feeding my obsession with the sounds Pauline made in the night. I could learn the private things Michael knew.

The first night, there was a campfire, and while we were supposed to be praying around it I studied Michael through slit eyes instead. We were all holding hands, palms clasped, but Michael and Pauline's fingers were intertwined. They did that sexy kind of hand-holding that involves all the fingers. I felt a great warmth that didn't come from the fire and a sudden and overwhelming desire to have Michael's tongue in my mouth. The thought of French-kissing Michael seeped into my prayers: *PleaseJesusjustoncepleaseJesus.* I was filled with guilt and weak with desire.

Somebody started a song:

It only takes a spark
to get a fire going
And soon all those around
can warm up in its glowing
That's how it is with God's love
once you've experienced it
You spread his love
to everyone
You want to pass it on

I loved this song. Michael sang it sometimes. The part about "once you've experienced it" was my favorite, because it sounded so coming-of-age, like a tampon commercial. There was something about singing it around a fire that was entirely too much. It was so sexy, and it made me feel like such a *teenager.*

And in that moment I felt almost calm, like maybe all I needed to make my thoughts slow down was the right man. This was a delusion that would affect my choices far into adulthood, but of course I didn't know that at the time. I just thought that someday, if I was good enough, if I was a good enough Christian, I could find a man like Michael, who would pull me close next to the fire and nestle his lips against my ear as he sang erotic Christian songs. Truth be told, I was having a little trouble differentiating between Michael and Christ Himself.

On my second day at camp, I became determined to save a soul, because I knew it was the thing that would make Michael proudest of me, and that when I told him what I'd done and we were rejoicing, he'd probably hug me, and I'd get to feel his strong arms around me and his breath in my hair. The opportunity to have one's soul saved occurred nightly as part of the scheduled activities, so I had to scout around for someone who was holding out, just waiting for me to be the link between them and the Messiah. So that evening, when we sat in assembly in the main hall watching films and singing songs and listening to the youth-specific sermon delivered by a hyperactive man with a skinny mustache who called himself Brother Brad, I was scanning the room for someone who looked reticent, someone who wasn't going forward to pray, cry, or be saved.

And I saw her: Erin. She was one of the very few people at Prairie Grove Middle School who made me look popular. She wore Toughskins jeans and heavy boys' clothes from Sears, even though it was summer. As we sat in church that night, she clutched beneath her armpit a paperback book with a robot on the front cover. When she blinked, her bangs moved a little, in a clump.

I realize, of course, the irony of my thinking I could save someone else. But all I wanted, all I had ever wanted, was a mission, direction. I wanted to know exactly what to do. There was nowhere else in my life where the rules were clear. They certainly weren't at home, where my father expressed anger by screaming and hitting, and my mother by ignoring me completely. I never knew what was going to set my parents off on any given day, and I never knew how to act at school. I walked around utterly terrified of saying or doing the wrong thing without realizing it. I was so bored and restless I could barely sit still, and I was always trying to contain my chants, to keep myself from moving my lips. Christianity, which is a paint-by-numbers religion if there ever was one, was perfect for me: you could always count on the Christians to tell you what to do.

The following morning, after a breakfast of reconstituted powdered scrambled eggs and warped white toast, I headed back to the cabin to find Erin. She had skipped volleyball, as had I, and she was wrapped in a *Star Wars* sleeping bag on her bed, reading a science fiction novel with a celery-stalk spine and no back cover.

"Hi Erin," I said, trying not to look directly at her.

She blinked. Her bangs made a quick movement back and forth.

"Ya wanna go for a walk?" I said.

She perked up. There was a slight shrug of her shoulders and one corner of her mouth pulled upward. She stood up from her bed, tucked her book under her arm, and followed me to the door, where I instinctively looked both ways for cool people before heading down a trail that led away from the cabins.

My heart was pounding. I wanted Erin to get to know Jesus, but I didn't want to be seen talking to her. In my imaginary version of the sky, Andy Warhol flew by in a Lear jet. He watched me through the lens of a Polaroid camera as I walked with this half-person half-mouse toward the gazebo, where she was to secure her place in Jesus' heart and my place in Michael's. Andy thought Bogg Springs was a very unsophisticated place to be, but to me it was the place where I might kiss Michael, so I ignored him.

"Erin," I said as we sat down, "there's something I've been wanting to talk to you about."

"Okay," she said, but it sounded like *okeeeee*, like a kazoo caught deep in her chest.

"I've noticed that you've been coming to church for a few months now, but you haven't gotten saved."

"Right." *Reeeeet.*

"Can I ask you why?"

She shrugged.

"Do you believe in God?" I asked.

"I don't know," she said, and it shocked me, because here was Erin admitting she might be an atheist and knowing full well that if she was and she died and she was wrong she would go to hell.

"I am here to tell you today that Jesus is real," I said. Brother Brad used that line a lot, and it seemed a fittingly dramatic response to the gravity of the situation.

"You think so?" Erin asked.

The question shot into the middle of me and did a little dance. Of course I thought so, because to think otherwise was

simply too scary. I believed in Jesus. Christianity was a talis-
man against all the things I was afraid of, and I often invoked
Jesus' name in the mantras I chanted to slow my thoughts: *I
askthesethingsinJesus'nameamenIaskthesethingsinJesus'name
amen* was a particular favorite. And here was Erin, who needed
mantras more than anyone as far as I could tell, who must
surely have words that rattled in her head to get her through
the day, and she was telling me she didn't believe in Jesus, and
she wasn't afraid.

"Yes," I said, "yes of course, I know so."

She nodded. "Okay."

I despised her with a white heat in that moment, hated her
for being braver than I was, and yet here she sat telling me
that, okay, sure, she'd get saved. I knew she was doing it to be
cool with me, just like I was saving her to be cool with Michael.
And yet I cried big Christian crocodile tears, pretending I was
sincerely happy I'd won a soul for Jesus, even though I had a
sneaking suspicion it was all bullshit.

Erin took my hand.

"We should probably pray now, right?"

She nodded in encouragement, scratching her armpit.

We prayed. I knew the prayer. I could say it by heart, but
it felt so broken and silly now, and the voices coming out of
my mouth belonged to Michael and my mother and Andy
Warhol but not to me. "Dear God," I croaked, "I am, uh,
here today with your child Erin, who recognizes that she has
not lived her life for You up until now. She has been living
for herself and that is wrong. She needs You in her life. She
believes that Your Son Jesus Christ gave His life for her on the

cross at Calvary, and she wishes to receive the forgiveness he made freely available to us through this sacrifice. Come into her life now, Lord. Take up residence in her heart and be her Savior, O Lord. From this day forward, she will no longer be controlled by sin, but will follow You all the days of her life. WeaskthesethingsinJeeziznameamen."

She brushed her bangs away from one eye, smiled, and pulled me to my feet. Then she started skipping, that is to say galumphing, like a horse, back toward the cabins. As she did, she launched into a loud chorus of "We're Off to See the Wizard," except she sang, "We're off to see the *Lo-ord*, the wonderful Lord of Heaven."

That night she sat with Michael for a long time and discussed the plans for her baptism when she got back to Prairie Grove. I sat three pews behind them in the chapel long after Brother Brad had finished his aerobic preaching and everyone else was singing around the campfire. I burned with jealousy as Michael's beautiful golden head touched Erin's greasy one, as he laid his hand across her back while they prayed. But I was also hopelessly proud of myself for having been the catalyst for this. If I couldn't be the girl he was touching, at least I had set him up with her. I couldn't get saved over and over, couldn't keep his hands on me all the time, but I could keep bringing greasy, pimply sheep into his fold.

As it happened, Erin was the only soul I ever saved. I wonder sometimes now if that means my bases are covered with the Christian God, if the insurance policy I bought myself through baptism, the one onto which I added Erin in the summer of 1984, might still through some loophole be in effect.

In the long insomniac nights now, which still occasionally come, when I'm anxious and slightly manic and getting flashbacks from the episode of *Little House on the Prairie* where Albert's girlfriend gets raped by a clown or the Elizabeth-has-a-poltergeist episode of *The Waltons*, where her Raggedy Ann doll walks by itself, I wonder whether Jesus is somehow still with me. Never mind the sex, drugs, and rock 'n' roll that have ensued, the cursing and kicking and punching in walls. Despite the years when I was a whirling dervish driven by my own deviant chemistry, maybe Jesus still has my back, still looks down on me and says, with an Arkansas accent, *It doesn't matter; I died for her sins, and when she was thirteen, she believed it for just long enough.*

4

IT ALWAYS AMAZES *me what people see in tattoos. I've been asked if the atoms on my arm are basketballs, if Dr. Caligari is Jerry Garcia, if Cesare the somnambulist is John Lennon. Denise has a heart pierced by a knife tattooed on each side of her chest, and although it's pretty obvious what they are, a woman walked up to her at a party one night and asked, "Are those balloons?"*

"No," said Denise. "Those are my breasts."

If Michael was the first man I desired, Owen was the first I craved with the intensity that makes you want to kick somebody or eat them or invent a new language to describe what they do to you. He lived across the street from my cousin Kendra, Linda's daughter, and they were friends. The summer fol-

lowing church camp, which is to say a few months before I
entered high school, Kendra turned sixteen and began to run
with the wilder side of the popular crowd; she was always riding around in some football player's Camaro or Cutlass and
telling me about what happened late at night at the end of that
summer when I still spent the night at her house. Although
Owen wasn't a football player, he was the wildest of the wild,
with a short rainbow Mohawk, and Kendra told me that he
often got "licks" at school, meaning that even though he was a
senior, he was still regularly paddled.

"What for?" I asked, mesmerized.

"Oh, you know. Skipping. Smoking. Blasting his music. He
likes to sit in his car in the parking lot at lunchtime and play
punk real loud."

Punk! Car! Cigarettes! Mohawk! Despite my devotion to
Jesus, I developed my first of many fervent crushes on rebellious
bad boys. I built up a mythology around him that involved the
two of us blowing Prairie Grove in his Mazda RX-7, his drawing table sticking out of the hatchback (Kendra had told me
he planned to study graphic design in college) and me in the
passenger seat wearing stylish round sunglasses and clutching
a scholarship to Oxford. In reality, I spent those summer days
lying in a sticky full-length lawn chair in my aunt's front yard,
slathered in baby oil up to the leg bands of my one-piece, too
insecure and pious to show my stomach, and waiting for Owen
to drive up in his little brown car with the too-loud muffler.

Sometimes, when he saw us outside, he would stroll over to
chat with Kendra about various parties on Eastwood Drive, the
neighborhood where the richest and most popular kids lived. I

tried at such moments to keep my mind on Jesus and his plan for me, the one Michael talked about on Sunday and Wednesday nights. I was hoping to be at least a little more popular that fall at school, which would give me the chance to witness to more people. I had recently taken a small leap in social status: I had won the Miss Clothespin pageant. I was excited about how my position as the princess of the Clothesline Fair would give me more of a platform to spread the word of God. I looked forward to the great honor of strolling through the booths of crafts and homemade candy wearing my tiara, my Aunt Pat's pink bridesmaid's dress from my Aunt Tessa's wedding, and, most of all, the satin ribbon sash that said *Miss Clothespin* in cursive letters made with gold glitter and Elmer's glue.

My mother had been thrilled that I wanted to compete. I was finally out of my room, not kneeling in front of the TV watching *The 700 Club* and praying for somebody's kidney. She took me to Hi-Lines, the nicest store in Fayetteville, and we bought a dress on sale. We got white pumps and pantyhose and L'Oréal ice-pink lipstick and nail polish at Montgomery Ward, and when I got home and tried it all on I felt like I could actually be pretty, maybe, if I just kept working at it. The Cyndi Lauper haircut was growing out and I had achieved a symmetrical chin-length bob.

I had prepared obsessively for the talent segment of the competition. I wrote a semiautobiographical story about my adventures with my cousin which I hoped the judges would see as an in-joke, since Kendra had held the title the year before. I memorized the story, illustrated it with Magic Markers on big pieces of Wal-Mart poster board, and delivered it as a monologue. I even spent the money I had earned that summer help-ing Kym Rutherford's family bale hay to buy a different outfit for the talent performance. I wore a yellow polo shirt, khaki shorts, and a matching green sweater vest and argyle socks. This was the same outfit the illustrated me wore in the poster-board drawings. I was proud of my attention to detail.

As I stood backstage breathlessly waiting to go on, clutch-ing my posters to my chest, I had prayed to God: *Please let me win, if it be Thy will, inJesus'nameamen.*

Onstage, I was a natural, hamming it up for my piano teacher, the basketball coach's wife, and the other judges from the Junior Civic League. It was the first time since I was a little girl inventing things in the backyard that I felt truly engaged, truly in my element, like I was doing what I had been put on earth to do.

And when I was announced the winner, it was one of the few times I have known something was about to go right for me. Kendra stood on the side of the stage holding the shining tiara, and when they called my name I laughed wildly as she placed it on my head. *Thank you, Jesus,* I said silently, hugging my cousin. *Thank you for finally making everything all right.*

I wanted to believe it was all right, because visions of nor-mal still danced in my head, and I still felt that, given my immediate environment, compulsive prayer was the best option I had for relief of any sort. So I stood that fall at the homecoming football game trying to be normal, wearing my glittery sash and a mum-and-pipe-cleaner corsage so big it had to be tethered to my sweater with four large straight pins. Miss Clothespin was required to wear the crown and banner at all major Prairie Grove events. My hair was long enough to be held back with black-and-gold barrettes, the same style as the girl on the cover of Beverly Cleary's book *Fifteen*. I tried to smile and look approachable for Jesus. Most of all, I tried to look like a teenager—*a real teenager*, not someone just on the verge of high school.

And approached I was, by the dreamy punk boy with a rainbow Mohawk, a boy with Clash patches pinned to his torn jean jacket, a boy who said, "Hey, Miss Clothespin."

Oh my god Owen. My heart raced, but I tried to remain casual as I leaned against the railing of the bleachers.

"Hey," I replied.

"So, you're Kendra's cousin, huh?" Owen asked, staring right at me, grinning a little with one side of his face, which was infinitely cooler than a full smile.

I nodded.

"I talked to her at school today," he said.

"Oh," I said, "really?"

"Yeah." He stared out at the football field, shifted his weight, looked back at me. "So do you want to go out sometime?"

I couldn't believe it. Owen was a *senior*. I was *fourteen*.

"Sure," I said. "You bet."

"Cool," he said, "Miss Clothespin."

And he took my hand, to shake it, to close the deal, but he lingered just a moment, and deliberately brushed his finger across my wrist. It felt so good, so lovely, so unlike anything I had ever felt before. It was better than singing the tampon song around the fire. It was *erotic*, I thought, the flash of the word through my head turning my face a bright crimson.

I wasn't sure what Jesus would think of Owen, so, later that night, I asked Him.

Lord, I said, *if it be Thy will, please let my parents let me go on a date.*

My mother was okay with it until she learned how old Owen was. But when I told her we were going to the Baptist church with his parents, who sang in the choir, and we were just friends, and I met him through Kendra, she consented. To this day I am amazed at that fact, but it happened.

Of course, we never went inside the church. We sat in Owen's car in the parking lot for a long time, talking about school, and Prairie Grove, and what it was like to live there after Little Rock, where he lived until tenth grade. He told me about a place called the Purple Cow where you could get purple milkshakes, and how much he missed them. I tried to burn the moment into my brain. We were sitting so close together. His new-car-smell air freshener was so grown-up and sexy.

Finally, he stopped talking, and he looked at me, and I looked at him, and he began that same slow lean forward I had seen so many times in the movies. With his lips millimeters from mine, I panicked.

"I don't know how to do this," I said, but he swallowed my words, and I closed my eyes and fell head over heels in love.

We continued to see each other throughout that fall. We made out a lot, but it was very chaste, mostly heavy kissing in various parking lots. For Christmas he bought me black-and-blue-checkered Zena jeans from the Jean Joint at the Northwest Arkansas Mall. I have a picture of myself wearing them at my grandma's house, opening presents, a bow from a package stuck to my head. I am smiling wildly. Both sides of my hair are the same length. I look like a happy girl.

And I was a happy girl; in fact, for about six months, I was deliriously happy. By night I made out with Owen at the top of Mount Sequoyah in Fayetteville, the lovers' lane overlooking the city where the glow of a bright blue lit-up cross cast watercolored shadows across the face of whoever was leaning in to kiss you. By day I went into the bathroom stall at school, between classes, and prayed that everything would last. It became a ritual: four times a day, I crouched on the toilet seat, bowed my head, and made sure I was still forgiven. After school I went to the video store where Owen worked and we watched horror movies and kissed.

One night we went to the mall and he studied me as I inhaled a cheeseburger and an Orange Julius.

"You always beat me when we're eating," he said.

"What?" I asked, mouth full, horrified.

"You always eat faster than I do. You eat as much as a guy. I've never seen a girl who eats as much as you."

"I'm hungry," I said, my cheeks on fire. I sensed that I had done something very, very wrong. I sensed that something was about to dramatically change.

He didn't answer. I slowed down. When he finished his fries, I still had some left. He looked at the wrapper and then up at me, and I got up to throw the fries away and he smiled approvingly. I wanted to dive into the trash can after them but I let them go, and was secretly sorry for their loss.

I began to eat at home before we went out so I could look more nonchalant about my food. I would have an apple and a large glass of water as I'd read about in one of my mother's magazines, which I now scanned for diets. I prayed for help, for guidance: *Please let me know what to do so he'll really truly like me. Please let me eat slower. Please give me the strength to get skinnier. I'll do anything if You'll just let the boy I like like me back.*

Anorexia starts as simply as that. Take the oversensitive girl in the "invalidating environment," as DBT therapists like to call it, and give her a boyfriend who tells her she's fat but he might love her if she wasn't, and you're off to a roaring start. My weight, I discovered, was something I could control, something I could adjust to garner approval from others. When Owen criticized my appearance, I did not get mad or tell him that was bullshit and that he needed to realize how awesome I was or hit the road. I had no idea that was something girls had the right to say. Instead, I panicked and begged.

"All you ever want to do is kiss," he said one night as we kissed. "I want to do other things sometimes."

"Like what?" Stricken with fear that he might leave me, I pleaded for him to tell me what was wrong.

"Well, I think you could stand to exercise. Maybe we should go ride our bikes or go for a run or something."

"I thought you liked to kiss me," I said.

"I'm kind of bored with just kissing," he replied.

"I'm not ready to do more than that."

"How do you know? You've never even tried."

"I just know," I told him. "It's wrong."

"Says who?"

"Says Jesus," I mumbled weakly. Somehow the argument seemed silly when I said it out loud.

"Jesus doesn't care," he said, and proceeded to put his hands up my shirt.

It continued that way for several weeks: he touched me, I protested, and he beat down my resistance until I gave in, tired from fighting and desperate for his love. At night, when I showered, I felt like I couldn't get clean enough, so I begged Jesus for forgiveness, for strength, and resolved not to let Owen touch me again.

And yet, I always did. It got so that we could no longer kiss without him fondling my breasts, squeezing them until my tiny size A fourteen-year-old nipples throbbed with pain. He kissed me hard when he did this, forcing his tongue into my mouth, something I didn't like nearly as much as I thought I would. Making out now meant a struggle to keep his hands within accepted boundaries.

Still, he stayed with me, he kept calling, so I knew that even if I wasn't doing right by Jesus, I was doing right by Owen. I tried writing him letters, long, loving missives detailing my passion for him, promising him that he would be The One, we just had to get married first. He put up with it for a while, but it made him grouchy. He made frequent comments about my weight, pointing out the parts of my body in which he could see its loss and the parts that needed work, and I found that I was frightfully turned on by seeing his large hands on my taut little belly, watching them take up more space day by day. He knew, when he slowed down, how to touch me, how to make me arch and ache and catch my breath, and the more weight I lost, the more deserving of pleasure I felt.

Anorexia takes hold fast. There is nothing more exquisitely painful, and for many years there was nothing that gave me so great a sense of accomplishment. It quickly became my best friend and worst enemy, like the beautiful cheerleader who bullies you but you put up with it because she lets you hang around with her. I was used to being bullied, so I had a particular strength for weakness—I felt comfortable admitting I was a lesser being and shrinking into my own shame. When I sat in front of a plate of French fries or a pizza, anorexia began to hiss at me: *You don't deserve it, fat pig. No girl eats as much as you.* And I replied, reflexively, *I know, I'm bad,* and I learned to push the plate away and swallow my drool.

Eating disorders don't take over unless you already feel you deserve less than other people, but if you do feel that way, they give you a strange power. They move in and simultaneously torment and protect you. They are a wonderful tool for helping you reject others before they can reject you. Example: You're at a party. The popular girls are there. You know you can never be as cool as they are, but when one of them pops a potato chip into her mouth or chooses real Coke over Diet, *for that moment* you are better. In denying yourself, you win. In deprivation of self, you are all-powerful. Ugly girls eat, pretty girls don't (or so anorexia's logic goes), and so for that one split second you are prettier. In the ten seconds or so it takes her to chew, you sit on the couch with your hands in your lap and your lip gloss perfect, and you know your closed-mouth smile is much nicer than hers, marred with chips.

I began to live for these moments of power, and to hammer at myself with the old familiar mantra first encountered in my mother's magazines: *Nothing tastes as good as thin feels.* There were midnight moments of truth, my hand on the freezer door with the ice cream just beyond it, when some sane part of me screamed *THIS DOES,* but most of the time I was able to walk away. I grew to love the feeling of saliva rising in my mouth in anticipation of food, because swallowing and denying myself made me feel so powerful. Never mind that in actuality I was growing weaker by the day, starting to get headaches at lunchtime when all I consumed was a massive glass of iced tea sweetened with calorie-free carcinogens from little pink packets, or that I was tumbling into bed at night weak and wobbly and racked with hunger pangs. Never mind that my intellect and my passions were rapidly being overtaken by this calorie-counting dictator who had taken up residence inside my head. It would be twenty years before I figured out that wide and winding is a lot more gratifying than straight and narrow.

One night in early spring, when his parents were watching Pat Robertson on TV in the next room, Owen took off my pants.

"Stop," I breathed, pushing hard against him, trying to find the strength to get away. Kissing was okay with God, hands on the breasts were iffy, but anything lower than that was definitely a sin.

"Shhh," he said, brave punk-rock knight to my shrinking-virgin princess. I knew I was giving in, knew I was gone. All I wanted, as he pulled my shirt over my head, was for him to see my flat belly, to run his palm across it, to pronounce me worthy. The air touched my bare breasts and my nipples hardened into crimson stupas. I craved him so badly, or rather, I wanted to feel his weight on me. I wanted to compare.

"Am I thin enough yet?" I asked.

"Almost," he said. "I can see your ribs. It's nice."

He rubbed against me for a bit, against my naked thigh, and I became warm between my legs, and slimy, the way he often left me. I secretly loved smelling my panties when I got home, because it was *his* scent, it was what he did to me. Nobody else made me smell that way. I could never tell him that, though; he'd think I was some kind of pervert. I felt how stiff he was inside his jeans and I sort of slid my hand between us and pressed my fingers against what I was pretty sure was the head of his dick. And then I remembered it was the last day of my period and I still hadn't taken out my tampon, and I lay there beneath him desperately scanning my mental database for what I knew of vaginas and sex, trying to figure out whether that would matter.

He pulled a box of condoms from his dresser drawer. I had only a vague idea what they were, and no clue how they actually worked. These condoms, apparently, were fruit-flavored, and they came in all different colors. I wasn't sure why anyone would need a flavored condom for birth control. Then I thought: *birth control.* I could get pregnant from this.

I sat upright. "I have to pee," I said.

"Okay," he panted. "I'll be ready when you come back. Be quiet."

I nodded and pulled on my shorts and slipped around the corner into the brown-wallpapered bathroom. I almost looked in the mirror, as had become my compulsion, lifting my shirt and pulling down my pants and examining everything from all angles at every conceivable opportunity. But I couldn't look, because the next time I saw myself, I wanted to be different. The next time I looked back at myself, I would be a changed woman. *I will have been* fucked, I thought, and it turned me on so much my knees went weak and I had to hang on to the sink. I lowered myself to the toilet but something felt locked inside me, the painful sensation of needing to pee but not being able to. I tried to rub myself with toilet paper to make it happen, but all I got was egg-white slime. I felt very, very dirty. I pulled out the tampon.

I walked through the living room on the way back to the bedroom, smiled at Owen's parents, and they nodded and smiled back at me. Owen's dad said "Amen!" in response to something on TV. When I tentatively pushed open the door, just a crack, I saw Owen kneeling on the bed with a big purple thing protruding from his pelvis. I almost screamed but then I realized it was the condom, the condom was purple. Grape. And he was touching it, and it looked like one of those Chinese water yo-yos filled with blood, something that should jump away from you if you tried to squeeze it in your hand. Which he was doing. Hard.

He grabbed me. He actually grabbed me, like in the movies, and he pulled me down on the bed and with his fingers separated the skin between my legs and I sucked in all my breath.

"Will I know when it's in?" I asked.

"Oh yeah," he said, "you'll know."

And then something hard forced its way inside me, like

being pounded with a rivet gun, and my stomach sucked all the way into my back. I curled like a roly-poly around this thing poking at my guts, my chitinous shell on the outside, all the raw pink-and-gray parts on the inside torn asunder.

I yelped, but his other hand was over my mouth before any sound could come out.

"Shhhh," he said into my neck, "shhh, it gets better."

I wrapped my lower lip around my bottom teeth and bit down hard. I made a vise grip that dug negative copies of my serrated incisors into the pink-flesh mold of my mouth. I squeezed my eyes shut until I saw my own lightning-bolt veins, red on black, and then he wrapped his arms around my back so my limbs flapped helplessly about his elbows, and one, two, three, he pushed into me, grabbing my shoulders and pulling me down hard around that swollen purple thing. There was a great tremble, a shuddering of boy, all hot breath and armpits and stubble, then everything went still and flat and quiet.

For a moment I thought he'd stopped breathing. All of him was on me, crushing me. Maybe he was dead. I didn't know or particularly care; I felt very far away, concerned only with looking at myself in the mirror as soon as possible. My friend Zoe's mom had a magnet on the fridge that said *Sex Burns Calories*, and I wanted to find out if it was true. I wanted to check the space between my thighs for the forty-seventh time that day to see if it had gotten any wider.

"Is it over?" I asked.

He heaved himself off of me and pulled off the condom, which hung limply, like a bruise, like an ink sack full of mimeograph fluid. He tossed it in the trash. He took off the album that was playing on the stereo: Oingo Boingo, his favorite band. *Dead Man's Party.* He did not answer.

"Okay," I said, because there was nothing else to say, "I guess I'll go."

He didn't reply. I didn't care. I pulled on my white cotton panties and white shorts, the size-5's I could finally wear after months of living on mostly canned green beans, chicken broth, and reduced-fat Club crackers. All I could think about was going home and looking in the mirror, standing on the bathroom counter, looking at the space between my legs where he had been.

I rode my bike home. It was a boys' ten-speed, the kind with the hard, skinny seat. By the time I'd pedaled the two miles back to my house, my white shorts were soaked with blood. Of course I was utterly horrified about how I was going to hide it. Luckily, thanks to anorexia, I was quickly becoming a master of hiding things.

My mother thought I'd been at Kendra's, and she was waiting up for me. I dashed into the bathroom, shoved a big wad of toilet paper between my legs, and began frantically scrubbing at my shorts. I could shove my underwear in the bottom of the trash can in the garage, but I had to get the stains out of my shorts.

I scrubbed until my fingers were frozen (I remembered from the menstruation film in fifth grade that cold water was best for getting out blood) and the bar of Ivory soap had turned bright pink. I kept watching in terror and praying as the blood swirls ran and hid in the pipes, washing away whatever it was Owen had done to me. *Please*, I begged, *please let it all come*

*out. I'll be good. I'll never do it again inJesus'nameamen, o gosh
o gosh o gosho.*

All the while, I snuck peeks at myself in the mirror—it
becomes a compulsion you can't stop, which is why I have no
mirrors in my house today—and nothing had changed. Absolutely nothing. I had always thought sex would involve wine
and roses and chocolate and lingerie. Or at the very least, the
guy taking his pants off all the way.

My mother knocked. I turned off the sink, threw the shorts
in the hamper, and sat on the toilet.

She came in. "Are you okay?"

"Yeah," I said, "I'm fine." I stared between my legs at the
lump of toilet paper and the red drips that fell into the toilet like
Easter egg dye. *Hippity hop,* I thought. *Here comes Peter Cotton-
tail.* My brain was turning cartwheels. "I just got my period."

Silence like drumbeats: five, six, seven, eight. Then she
said it.

"I thought you just had your period." "Did you start again?"

"Why would you ask that?" I tried to think of a legitimate
answer, I really tried, but what did I know about bodies that
I could pull over on my mom? Instead, I just started crying,
hoping for pity and/or mercy, whatever I could get.

I have never seen her look at me like that. Everything she
had hoped for me was shattered right then, as I sat on the toilet
weeping. All the words mothers and daughters usually offer
one another were not available to us, because we were terrified of each other, and because sex was not a hot topic in the
Pershall household. I couldn't look at her. Eventually she shut
the door and never asked again.

He broke up with me the next day.

Here, though, the story diverges from that told by a million girls jilted by a million lame guys. Here is where the eating disorder ascends the throne and tells me what to do, and the Dog and I obey with bowed head and tucked tail. Here is where I feel so dirty, so wrong, that I give up membership in the human race, where the sound in my brain becomes a constant screech of metal on metal, as if I am a self-punishment machine and someone has pulled my string, wound my key, set me on the track, and I chug straight on down the path full speed ahead.

I couldn't allow myself to eat like normal people anymore, ever, because they were humans and I was a dog. I had to take my food into my bedroom and eat it on all fours. I was not allowed utensils, and for a while I think I actually forgot how to use them. I could eat French-cut green beans, out of a bowl, on my hands and knees. My water had to come from a bowl, too, because lapping was especially degrading. I had to be punished for every ounce of fat that remained on my body and every time I had let Owen touch me. The atonement had a very specific ritual. First, I had to write on the fat parts with markers, and the Bad Dog would chant in my head and tell me what to write. If someone said something mean to me that day, I had to record it on my flesh. So when I stood looking in the bathroom mirror one day at school and Kyra walked in with two of the other cheerleaders, I could just feel her looking me over, and I knew that night the punishment would be extreme.

"Gosh, Stacy," she said, "you have so many blackheads your nose looks like a strawberry."

This is the kind of idiotic bullshit high school girls say, but at the time it meant that I would huddle in my closet after everyone else had gone to bed, marker across my face, sucking chicken broth out of a saucer, breaking the surface of the soup with my tears. I did this late at night, after my parents had gone to bed. For a while, it was easy to fool them; we all liked to eat different things so we tended to be responsible for our own meals rather than sitting down at the table together. This meant that, at least in the beginning, I could get away with it. I could take the Sharpie off my face with nail polish remover before they woke up, park myself at the kitchen table with my homework, and tell them I'd already had breakfast.

I needed the sting of the polish remover on my skin to feel forgiven, cleansed: acetone atonement. I needed to hit myself in the head in my closet, needed to beat out of me the part that had failed everyone so completely. Most of all, I needed the scratch in my throat when I cheated, when I ate more than I was supposed to, when I broke down and binged in the dark and my fingers tripped over themselves to find that little piece of cartilage behind my tongue, the one that brings it all up when pressed. Oh yes; I found bulimia after Owen left me. As far as I'm concerned, once you start puking, you're a goner. The eating disorder has taken over. All you are is one big alimentary canal, like an earthworm, existing only for the purpose of playing with your food.

So I hit and I wrote and I barfed and I lapped and somehow still it was never enough. Somehow I still kept waking up inside myself.

5

IN 1877, THOMAS EDISON *decided to create a talking doll by implanting a phonograph in her chest. Ten years later, another inventor named William W. Jacques developed a prototype based on Edison's design. The doll was almost two feet tall and sold for ten dollars at Schwarz's Toy Bazaar, in New York City's Union Square. Edison later said that "the voices of the little monsters were exceedingly unpleasant to hear."*

In 2004, Denise's friend Emma Porcupine tattooed a pink-haired version of this doll on my left arm, from wrist to elbow. Emma referred to her as "the brain eater," and she does indeed look like she might very possibly eat brains. She has tiny pearl teeth, curly pink hair, and Mary Janes with bows. She is naked, and her torso is opened up to reveal her mechanical innards.

Emma gleefully imitates her, clicking her teeth and saying,
"Brains! Braaaaaiiins." And once again I am thrilled to have found
another strange girl, another beacon, another one who gets it.

Throughout my childhood, Zoe Maxwell was the closest
thing I had to a best friend. She lived in my neighborhood,
was in my class at school, and actually liked me most of the
time, for which I was profoundly grateful. In high school, her
brother became a big football star, which meant that being
friends with Zoe was as close to popular as I would ever get.

Her family's house smelled like perm solution, Giorgio perfume, and unwashed FryDaddy. Her mother worked at the
JCPenney hair salon, but to earn extra money she gave cuts
and perms at home to the ladies who didn't want to drive all
the way to Fayetteville. One afternoon while a perm sizzled on
a local woman's head in the utility room, Zoe and I attempted
to sway the house's olfactory balance in the direction of the
FryDaddy, into which Zoe tossed several Schwan's frozen
hamburger patties.

"Do you think it'll work like this?" I asked, taking a giant
whiff of grease. It smelled so delicious I wanted to dive in, but
I was already calculating the calories and figuring out how I
would get rid of them.

"Hell yes," she said. "It's just like putting them on a grill,
except in oil."

Like much of Zoe's logic, I wasn't sure exactly what this
meant. As the beef pucks sizzled away, I stood in the doorway of the den with the remote control of the VCR, rewinding
Janet Jackson's "Pleasure Principle" video over and over again

to watch the part where she steps on the chair and tips it over. "We have to practice this part," I said, tugging at my knee-pads. We'd been working on it in the garage for weeks, because Zoe wanted to make the drill team and I wanted to still be her friend once she did.

"I need some kneepads like yours," she said, because she'd been using her brother's old football ones, and mine were sleek new neoprene.

"Wal-Mart," I said absently, as if everything in her house and mine didn't come from Wal-Mart, just like every posses-sion of everyone else we knew. Of course, many of my clothes came from garage sales, to which my mother went every Sat-urday at 6 a.m., and I lived in fear someone might ask me why my new polo shirts had already been washed so many times.

"Motherfucker!" said Zoe, whose family had the biggest collective dirty mouth in Prairie Grove. "The burgers are fall-ing apart."

We fished them out of the FryDaddy and Zoe had the bril-liant idea of smooshing them into meat loaf. She wasn't exactly sure of the recipe, but knew it involved crumbled-up bread or chips or something, so she mashed in some Nacho Cheese Dor-itos and drowned the whole thing in ketchup. I couldn't believe I was really going to eat it, but god it smelled so good, meat fried in oil with ketchup and orange powdered cheese, and if it was all I ate for the next two days and I exercised for two hours a day, I figured I should be able to get rid of it. I could get through up to two days without food as long as I had enough iced tea, coffee, and sugar-free gum. I made up my mind that the next time I would eat would be Saturday, when I worked my part-time job at the Skate Place in the snack bar, where my usual binge was three rectangular frozen sausage pizzas cooked in the toaster oven, all the cotton candy I wanted, two 32-ounce drinks made of every kind of soda mixed together, and popcorn soaked in extra butter-flavored grease to make it easier to purge. For some reason I had decided I need to bring saltine crackers with me from home to eat in the midst of all this, because eating disorders are nothing if not bizarre combinations of ritual and specific foods. I would eat the pizza, then slam down half of one of the sodas, then eat a cracker, then purge. Then cotton candy and half a soda and two handfuls of popcorn and a cracker and then purge. Yes, that was what I would eat on Saturday afternoon.

"Hey asshole," said Zoe, "stop thinking about sex. Do you want some of this?" I nodded and blinked and she used a large wooden spoon to glop some coral-colored Dorito meat onto a plate, which she shoved at me. If you asked me what I learned during my high school career, I would struggle to come up with something about cotton gins or gerunds and the meaning of *synecdoche,* but I will be able to describe that meat loaf in grueling detail until the day I drop dead. Food, hunger, food, hunger, food: this was my life. What food tasted like going down, what it tasted like coming up. What I ate in what order, how many calories it had. I remember calculating how many times I would have to chew each Dorito bit so it wouldn't stab my throat on the way back up, and I remember how they looked like shards of broken pottery sticking out of the oily, ketchupy meat.

"This tastes like shit," Zoe proclaimed with the first forkful, and the brakes slammed on in my stomach, an automatic response to anyone eating less than or slower than me. So I pretended I didn't like it either. I swallowed my saliva and hoped it was not obvious that what I really wanted was to eat it all, lick the FryDaddy clean, and suck the rest of the ketchup from the squeeze bottle.

"Let's go practice," I said, pushing the plate away.

In the summer of 1986, Zoe lived, ate, slept, and breathed Janet Jackson, which meant I tried over and over to put my right foot on the seat of a chair, my left foot on the back, tip the whole thing over, and slide across the floor in a kneeling position. Granted, pastel-fabric-covered *Golden Girls*-era kitchen chairs with bows and skirts were not the best vehicles for this move, but they were all we had, so we keep trying.

"If I don't make the fucking drill team, I'm gonna be so pissed," said Zoe, wiping the sweat from her brow.

"Yeah, totally," I echoed, but the truth is that I didn't really give a damn about the drill team per se. I cared about losing weight, being skinny, and not losing Zoe. She was a good dancer, and her brother was a popular football player, and she would undoubtedly make the team. This was the inevitability toward which we had been slouching for years, the moment I had dreaded. This is where Zoe and I would irrevocably split off into The Popular One and The Smart One. This was high school, where we were at last forced to stand definitively on opposite sides of the line.

When the day of tryouts arrived, Zoe and I joined thirty other girls in dancing around the gym to Janet and Haircut 100, and I forgot to smile. I lost my smile in increments my sophomore year—week by week, pill by pill, purge by purge, green bean by green bean, I felt it sliding down my face and disappearing. I learned that it's very hard to smile and remain vigilant in your self-punishment at the same time. I could barely keep up with the calories in things. I didn't have time for facial expressions. I had more and more energy but less and less personality every day, every time I threw up. Written in red on my critique sheet: *No smile.*

Zoe smiled a lot. As I knew she would, she made drill team. I did not.

It is as easy as that to put a fence between girls. Zoe, my best friend since we were five, jumped overnight into an echelon of popularity reserved for blond girls rich enough to keep their tans all year. All the cheerleaders came back from lunch smelling like tanning beds, drinking Diet Coke out of Big Gulp cups, and now Zoe would too.

I would go to her house still, sometimes, when she wasn't at practice or performing at a ballgame, and I would touch her uniforms when she went to the bathroom. One night I even held her huge poofy pom-poms and stood in front of her mirror, wondering if I was skinny enough to deserve to be holding them, and then, tentatively, I sat at her dressing table and arranged the pom-poms around my face, striking the pose in which the spirit squad were photographed for the yearbook. I knocked her curling iron off the table and it landed, plugged in and scorching, in my lap. I jumped up screaming, because it stuck to me; Zoe had a habit of rolling her bangs around it and then spraying the whole thing with hairspray, and she did this so many times a day she saw no need to ever turn the thing off. The flesh on my thigh went up in a broiling haze of JCPenney-salon-brand product commingled with the aroma of steak. I threw down the pom-poms, the curling iron landed on top of them, and they started melting too. By the time Zoe came running, I was hopping around hooting in a room that reeked of burning plastic and seared flesh, and she shrieked and dove to save her pom-poms.

Note to self: You are not as important as plastic. This is how you will see it, and she will see it as you being jealous and sabotaging her stuff. And you will part, and you will miss her almost as much as you miss food, but thankfully, not quite. And this, this is how an anorectic survives hell: it will all be okay as long as nothing in the world is *quite* as important as food. You can coast for a long time on that one. Too long.

Eventually Zoe started acting like she didn't want to be seen with me. Granted, I had, not long after drill-team tryouts, chopped off all my hair and taken to wearing my eyeliner like Alex in *A Clockwork Orange,* so there was that. Tenth grade was the year my mother asked me more days than not if I was a lesbian, a drug addict, or a Satan worshiper, and she meant it. I just figured that if I was going to look scary, I might as well look *really* scary. It was like playing Celia, I needed the accoutrements. I needed the big black sweaters and the fucked-up black hair and the clunky black shoes and the matching black attitude. I needed the weird T-shirts, the weird books, the weird music, and the otherwordly thinness. I wasn't just playing Disease anymore, I was playing Anorexia, and I was by god going to be good at it. I was doing it so it felt real, to paraphrase my newfound idol Sylvia Plath.

For a while I really believed it was just that: playing. I was toying with the idea of sickness, flirting with it, but because I was not yet what I would consider emaciated, I felt I could give it up at will and move on to something else. The old I-can-quit-anytime-I-want. But soon I was sort of playing but it was sort of real, and then it was entirely real and I realized it had never been a game at all. Playing with anorexia is like playing with heroin, fire, plutonium, or Scientology—it's just a bad idea all around. Playing with anorexia is like cracking open mercury thermometers and drinking them just to see what happens. Anorexia, to use the vernacular, ain't playin'.

THIS IS WHERE Lula Vandeventer enters the story, or, perhaps I should say, reenters. When Lula first moved to Prairie Grove from Tulsa, Oklahoma, she had impressed me with the fact that she was being raised by her gay uncle (though nobody ever used the word "gay"), had an exotic, lovingly cultivated Valley Girl accent, and was missing the pinkie toe on her left foot, having lost it in a terrible accident with her uncle involving something called a Vespa. I didn't completely trust her; she was one of those girls who always had to one-up everybody, especially when talking about her family. She talked about all the vacations she'd taken, all the exotic alcoholic beverages she'd tried, and how her four-year-old brother was a certified genius. One night, all those years ago when we were all just twelve, she had invited me and Zoe to spend the night at her house.

My first inkling that all was not right came when I met her little brother. In truth, Tymythy, who had been named by and startlingly resembled the uncle in a tangle of parentage I could never quite unravel, was not so much a genius as a shrill, beady-eyed fruit bat of a child, constantly swooping from place to place and never shutting up. His favorite thing to talk about was himself; specifically, his abilities in comparison to those of popular film and television characters. "I can run faster than Nanny Gann can," he said, referring to the heroine of a popular Disney movie whose name was actually *Natty* Gann, and he said it over and over again and his uncle said it too.

"Oh, yes, Tymythy," cooed Alec Zander Vandeventer, a towering, oversized man with an oppressive hairdo—a sort of cotton-candy copper-orange concoction, a going-for-blond-but-can't-quite-get-there look—who stomped through the house like an impending thunderstorm or indignant wildebeest. "You *can* run faster than Nanny Gann can!"

This right here is a great way to drive an anorexic spelling and grammar fiend crazy: Say something wrong, and say it with authority. Revel in your own damn ignorance. My id was running circles around itself wanting to scream out to them *Goddammit it's not fucking Nanny, it's NATTY,* and in my head a relentless chant began: *nattynotnanny, nattynotnanny, nattynotnanny.* But I knew that correcting other people's uncles was not something you did, so I sat at the kitchen table grinding my teeth and tapping my foot instead. I had twelve long hours before I could go home.

Later that night, Lula incorrectly used the word "fetish," and Alec Zander Vandeventer practically shot out of his chair to issue a correction. "Fetish," he said, "f-e-i-t-i-s-c-h. Fetish. It means something weird that gives you sexual pleasure." As the word "sexual" crossed his lips, he let out a loud bellowing snort-laugh, like a wounded hyena.

"Wait," I said, with a red blood swell behind my eyes, unable to take it any longer, trying to keep from kicking him or vomiting all over him or something. "How did you just spell it?"

"F-e-i-t-i-s-c-h," he replied, looking at me authoritatively over the tops of his bifocals like a goddamn college professor. *College professor of crap*, I thought, somewhat shocked by this agitated fury that was coming to own me. When he moved his head, his hair followed in one unyielding piece, an independent inanimate object just along for the ride.

"That's . . . not . . . how . . . you . . . spell . . . it," I said, slowly, evenly, measured so as not to unleash the Bad Dog. My vision narrowed into that little red tunnel of self-righteous rage. "Fetish is spelled f-e-t-i-s-h."

"Horse testicles," said Alec Zander Vandeventer, snorting.

I shot backward through the red tunnel, so taken aback that he had just said *horse testicles* that I went upstairs and avoided him for the rest of the night. I sat in the corner of Lula's room and counted things: my breaths, my taps, the number of calories in four Club crackers, whatever. I pretended I was looking at magazines, but really I was counting. This caused Lula to stop speaking to me, which meant Zoe couldn't speak to me either because it was Lula's house, and they were preteen girls doing what so many before them had done to so many others. I spent the night huddled on a love seat beneath an acrylic granny-square afghan in the downstairs living room, exiled, cast out in that way that only junior high girls can cast one out—and, like generations of outcasts before me, I lay there in the dark by myself thinking I was the only one. I couldn't see then that I was one of millions of girls going through the exact same thing, so I internalized the rejection: *It's all me, there's something wrong with me, if I weren't fat/ugly/stupid/ whatever, they wouldn't treat me this way.* For some reason, I still insisted on considering both of them friends—in Zoe's case, because she acted differently when we weren't around Lula, and in Lula's because I was too scared not to. I didn't want to be on her or her uncle's bad side. Friendship by way of terror: at twelve, I already knew it well.

Not long thereafter, Lula bleached her hair white-blonde and grew such enormous tits that everyone started calling her Charo. As such, she secured at least a moderately respectable position in the Prairie Grove social hierarchy, even though she wasn't on the spirit squad. She became, instead, the girl with the muscle car who drove the spirit squad around and bought them all cigarettes and beer with her fake ID, with help from her ample bosom.

And so, in high school, Zoe and Lula became close, and I clamored behind them still trying to be their friend, pretending to like whatever they liked so they would include me. Of course, in truth, I found Lula loathsome and wanted nothing to do with her, but the eating disorder, the punisher, seized the opportunity to sign me up for more abuse—which would, of course, fuel more weight loss.

Lula had always been, quite blatantly, one of those girls who felt delight in her very circulatory system at making other girls suffer—not just me, but anyone who pissed her off in any way. Again, one of a million bullies in a million schools doing the same thing to a million other girls with low self-esteem. Like all bullies, she took offense at the slightest infraction and sought revenge at all costs. It was not at all uncommon to enter the building one morning and find that, while you slept, you had become Lula's worst enemy for no reason you could discern—perhaps your jeans were nicer than hers, or you had spoken to a boy she liked. She thrilled to the plaintive voices of the girls who followed her down the halls begging for an explanation. But Lula Vandeventer gave them none, leaving them to moan and wail and beg for her forgiveness.

Or, at least *I* moaned and wailed and begged for her forgiveness. She heard *my* plaintive voice. I could walk through the halls of Prairie Grove High School looking like a reject from A Flock of Seagulls and pretending to be a badass, but the truth was that I still went home, sat in the closet, and wrote Lula's and Zoe's insults on my body with markers at night, huddled in my closet sobbing atop a pile of shoes. I curled myself into the familiar uncomfortable, humiliated ball, closed the door, and by the glow of the desk lamp coming through the slats I wrote on my arms and legs *STUPID. FAT. BAD DOG.* And then, after the rest of the family had gone to bed, I crawled out, made myself a bowl of chicken broth, and slurped it on my hands and knees.

It is obvious that I was an easy target. The slightest thing could set me to trembling and apologizing, could ignite the engine of impulse. It took so very little—less and less the weaker I got from the eating disorder. I wanted friendship, wanted acceptance, wanted to get invited to parties, but as the social chasm between me and the other girls widened, I saw those things slipping further from my grasp. I didn't want to be alone. I had to have some kind of friends, and Lula and Zoe were the closest thing I had. When there is nothing to eat but bread and water, bread and water look good.

I implored them to like me, and they gleefully refused, for reasons known only to girls between the ages of nine and eighteen. At one point, having saved up my Skate Place money, I bought a pair of Zena jeans that buckled in front instead of zipped, but the buckles didn't work so well. They had a tendency to pop open, and Zoe and Lula decided that I bought the jeans knowing this, because I wanted attention, as if having a maddeningly inoperable fly was a way to win friends and influence people. This was an offense punishable by three days of being completely ignored. Once, Lula looked at my copy of *The Andy Warhol Diaries*, the one I carried around all year, and said, "He's *gay*. Are *you* gay?" while Zoe looked on and snickered. Behind the snicker, I saw terror in her eyes, the fear that Lula would turn on her if she didn't. In that moment, although I felt betrayed, I forgave her. I still loved her and wouldn't have wished Lula's wrath on anyone.

Everything I did right was, in effect, wrong. If I won an award, I was a snob. If it was announced that I had gotten the only A in English, I was an attention hog. And every day that this continued I went to school sicker and sicker at the thought of seeing Lula's smug, biscuity face when I walked through the door. I fantasized about running her over with a tractor or ratting her out to the liquor store, and these thoughts brought me comfort. But more than anything, I just wanted to be invited to somebody's party. I wanted to be one of the girls who were allowed to pile into Lula's car at lunch hour. I fantasized about impressing the spirit squad with my ability to not eat. I imagined going to Tastee Freez and watching them all eat chicken nuggets and French fries with ranch dressing while I smiled and sipped my aspartame iced tea. Then I fantasized about chicken nuggets and French fries with ranch dressing.

Sometimes things were still okay with Zoe and there was a reprieve, and I was momentarily as close as I got to happy. But most mornings I arrived at school wondering what grave unknown infraction I had committed the day before, and when she and Lula wrote notes to each other in study hall I knew, just *knew*, that they were writing about me. My paranoia skyrocketed, my weight continued to plummet, and I hid in my own world as much as possible, occupying my mind with numbers, trying to see those numbers as made of fat and dripping off my body.

It should come as no surprise that tenth grade was the first time I tried to kill myself. Well, not technically—it was more like the first time I wrote a note and chickened out. But once I had known the idea, rolled it around on my tongue and tasted its battery-acid truth, I knew it was for me. It was the relief I sought; I dug my toes into suicide like cool wet sand after a walk on hot pavement. I was now a girl with a Secret, and the secret was that I was going to die. I just had to find the right time to announce it. (Being borderline and all, *not* announcing it was not an option.)

I nurtured my obsession with every book and movie about every fucked-up girl I could find. I fell in love with Anne Sexton, read *The Bell Jar* approximately eighty million times, and grew my bangs long in my face to hide my eyes. I devoured every electroshock scene in any medium. I told myself over and over: *Well, this is it, I'm going crazy, I'm just like Sylvia Plath, I'll be dead soon.* I toyed with how I might do it: head in the oven (too copycat), overdose (where would I get the pills?), wrist-slitting (my mother would never get the blood out of the grout), jumping in front of a car (the speed in Prairie Grove was 40 miles an hour, how much damage could that do?). I tried to drown myself in the bathtub a few times, just to see if I could do it, but at a certain point my body forced my head up out of the water and breath into my lungs, pissing me off greatly.

The day I finally wrote my suicide note and went home to carry out my threat was the day of Quiz Bowl tryouts. Unlike drill team, which I never really expected to make, I fully anticipated a slot on the Quiz Bowl team. I demanded absolute perfection from myself when it came to intellectual pursuits. I had been pouring books into my head all year, going down the official U.S. Quiz Bowl Recommended Reading List and checking off *The Scarlet Letter, The Sound and the Fury, Moby-Dick, For Whom the Bell Tolls.* In an effort to indicate just how literate I was, I mail-ordered an F. Scott Fitzgerald T-shirt, which of course served as one more roadblock between me and cool.

What stood in the way of my Quiz Bowl glory was Farley Anderson: history teacher, Baptist preacher, and insane Vietnam vet. Mr. Anderson and I despised each other, although, because he was a teacher and I wanted to be on the Quiz Bowl team, we pretended to get along. But I became meaner, nastier, and more high-and-mighty with every day I starved myself, which meant I just had to open my mouth and say something when he consistently skipped everything in our textbook that had to do with art and instead found a way to make all of U.S. history about the Vietnam War. His face and ears would turn bright red, his pupils would shrink, and I would sit at my desk with my arms crossed, staring him down, daring him to challenge me. The more banned books I read, the more the Jesus thing slipped away, and the fact that Mr. Anderson so fervently believed it even though he was several decades older than me began to drive me nuts. For as timid and wheedling as I was with Lula and Zoe, I could be a mouthy pain in the ass with Mr. Anderson. He had a habit of always calling us "children"; had, in fact, a habit of nicknaming everyone. For example, he always referred to a bus driver named Jim as "Bigness," for no reason that any of us could discern.

Being in Vietnam had done something to his eyes. They were beady and shifty and darted about beneath his sweaty crimson forehead as he expounded at length about weaponry. On Sundays he stood in the choir loft at the Baptist church wearing a blue satin robe and a white collar that was too tight around his neck, and this seemed to make his eyes dart about even more. I would stand in the pews, increasingly bored, watching him pronounce the word "iron" EYE-ron because it had a dash in it in the hymnal, and then he'd realize his mistake and his eyes would ricochet like pinballs to see if anyone had heard him.

Mr. Anderson was in charge of the Quiz Bowl team because

he was the only Advanced Placement teacher at our school. He was the teacher they stuck you with if you were "gifted and talented." Our ongoing battle of wills came to a climax one day when he finally stopped to talk to my AP history class about "one of the important artworks" mentioned in our American history book: *The Vietnam Memorial*. The previous week he'd skipped over the American expatriate writers and artists, dismissing them by scorning their decision to leave the United States and calling them Communists. We didn't have time, he said, to cover the art stuff in the book anyway. This week, thoroughly pissed off, I couldn't help challenging him. I asked him why art was important all of a sudden.

He looked at me, froze his freaky ice-blue eyes on me, his comb-over and his face the same shade of red, and he hissed, "I'll tell you one thing, child, this means a hell of a lot more than a little bit of paint thrown on a canvas."

I jumped up and ran out the door of the classroom, down the hall, and into the bathroom, locked myself in a puke-green stall (appropriate), balled up my sweater in my fists, and screamed into it as loudly as I could. This is one of the first blinding red rages I remember, the ones that would become more and more frequent as the BPD progressed, one of the first times my response to injustice was so out of control that the bottom dropped out from under me like the world was a Gravitron and I was plastered to the wall. I had never seen anyone besides my father experience rage to this degree, and it terrified me: girls weren't supposed to get this mad. It was one of two times Mr. Anderson would rouse these feelings—the second time, I would try to kill myself.

Everybody else seemed to like him, to find him funny, and I felt even weirder because I could see through him, and he was an adult. Still, I wanted to be on Quiz Bowl, and Mr. Anderson was the one who graded the placement test. I knew I had to get control of myself and attempt a smooth relationship with him, even if I had to fake it just like I was doing with Lula. He had to choose four students for the team, one for English, one for math, one for science, and one for history and geography. We were all supposed to be well-rounded, but we were supposed to have a "specialty" as well. Because placement on the team was ostensibly based on this score alone, I was hoping that I would get everything right on the English to make up for my poor math skills. After all, I'd gotten perfect scores on the ACT and SAT in English, but was more excited to earn an "average" on the math; this meant I could go to college.

So it was that I walked into the Quiz Bowl test one May afternoon, knowing full well that the person who made and would be grading it viewed the whole of world literature as the pursuit of Commie pinko tree-huggers. I shouldn't have been surprised when I bombed.

I got a 73 on the test, which was five pages of math, a few obligatory questions about books and verb conjugation, and three final pages of questions about various wars. When Mr. Anderson handed the test back to me and I saw the big red number, the Bad Dog came wailing up through me and my tears burned my eyes. I ran out of the room and down the hall to my locker, grabbed my notebook, went out the back door, and kicked the building over and over again until I realized

I could break my legs or have a heart attack, at which point I collapsed on the ground and tried to scream but only sobbed.

When I caught my breath I flung open my notebook and began to write my suicide note. But rather than directing it to Mr. Anderson, or even my family, I directed it to Zoe and Lula. I said that I was sure they wouldn't even remember me by next week, but if they did, to please think of me as the girl who only wished she could have been good enough for them. Knowing how bad such a thing could make them feel for the rest of their lives sent a delicious surge of power and terror through me, like when you bite your tongue in your sleep and wake up tasting your own blood. Manipulative suicidal ideation: I know that here, if not previously, it is safe to say I was definitely borderline. (Every time I label myself as such, part of me feels as though I'm buying into the sort of psychobabble—I hate that word, by the way—that fills the self-help section at chain bookstores, as well as the tendency of middle-class folks in the Western world to pathologize damn near everything, but it's true. The diagnosis applies, and here is where it began, without a doubt, to do so.)

I knew as I stuffed the note through the slats of Zoe's locker that I had to make everybody think I meant to die—again with the manipulation—and that a grand dramatic gesture had to be made. Once again, I was limited by geography. There was no place to make grand gestures in Prairie Grove. I wanted to steal a car and drive off a cliff, but there were no cliffs and everybody knew everybody else's car.

I had a pocketknife on my keychain, and I knew I had to at least cut myself up a little bit. I was alone, I could have done it a thousand times over. I pulled into the driveway of my house but I didn't get out of the car. My mother was out, my dad was on the truck, I could have done it. I could have really truly cut myself and died before anyone came home. But when I tried to press the knife hard enough against my wrist to break the skin, I couldn't. I made a series of tiny kitten-claw scratches. I slumped down in the seat and hated myself for still being alive, for being so goddamn weak.

As I sat trying to summon the courage to do it again, *really* do it, slit my wrists like someone with some balls and not scratch at myself like a petulant child, Lula's car came squealing up behind me. Zoe leapt out of the passenger seat, ran over to my car, started pounding on the window, and screamed to Lula. "Oh my god, she's here. She's okay. She's alive."

"You fucking baby!" shouted Lula, running up behind her.

We yelled and swore at each other. They loved me, they said. I said, You don't. If you loved me, I said, you wouldn't give a shit about the jeans I wore. You wouldn't care that I wasn't on drill team. You wouldn't tell me I was getting skinny just because I wanted attention.

You're just paranoid, they said, and dramatic. Don't forget dramatic.

That afternoon, as I sniveled for forgiveness, I begged them not to take the note to the principal. They begged me to "get help, because, like, you seriously need it." And I realized the most terrifying truth of all: I was no longer fighting with other girls. It had gone way beyond that. Somewhere things had shifted, and now I was fighting my own war, inside my own head. I didn't need other people at all anymore. It was just me and anorexia, all alone.

Of course, Zoe and Lula didn't speak to me the next day at school. It didn't really matter. I was free to be as fucked up as I wanted, and there was no small measure of relief in that.

I restricted my food intake to five items: green beans, chicken broth, canned white chicken, water-packed tuna, and saltine crackers. I stole individual packets of crackers from the school cafeteria and carried them to work in my backpack. I'd eat a couple, throw up, eat a few more, repeat. I never allowed myself to eat more than three crackers without barfing. Which meant, of course, that on occasion it was okay to eat half the Skate Place snack bar before the three crackers. Some nights I ran the soda machine out of syrup.

My already-oversized dresses got baggier as I slid from 140 pounds to 110. By December of my sophomore year, I weighed just over 107 at five foot six, which bothered me because it was not an even number. I was convinced that once I hit 98 everything would be perfect: people would like me, Owen would come back and beg for my forgiveness, and I'd be the skinniest girl in school. Ninety-eight was the magic number. I bought some sneakers and started waking up at 5 a.m. to run.

I beat out chants in my head in time with my footsteps as I jogged around the gravel track at the park. I didn't have to make them up; my hungry, sleep-deprived brain was a font of bizarre word combinations and rhymes. This is a condition of hypomania, which, for me, is a strong indication that BPD is not actually a personality disorder but a mood disorder, and rightfully deserves a place on the bipolar spectrum. The more I ran, the more I starved, the more entire elaborate poems began to form themselves without my conscious effort. One trait of the bipolar brain is its facilty with wordplay.

In preparation for the day when I broke 100 pounds, I had bought myself a pair of size 3 forest-green pants. They were folded lovingly in the bottom drawer of my dresser, and I would occasionally open the drawer and stroke them, or take them out and drape them across my lap. This was a favorite tactic to use when I was hungry. The pants became a symbol of the perfect life that was only nine pounds away, and my starving nervous system drummed out an early-morning ode to them as I leaned into hill after hill:

You . . . will . . . make it around
You will . . . lose . . . nine pounds
You will . . . wear . . . the green . . . slacks
Before you know, you'll be looking back

Slacks. Like anyone who was sixteen years old ever used that word. But I will never forget the chant. And underneath its rhythm, the bilious rumblings of my indignant empty stomach. These sounds can be swirled together.

Here is what people with eating disorders do: We pick foods at random and adorn them with meaning. If, for example, one eats exactly one-half can of fat-free chicken broth with exactly two saltine crackers at 12:37 p.m., one can then eat half a can of green beans at 4:19 and then the other half at 8:42, and all will be right with the world. God forbid one should be delirious from diet pills and lack of sleep, and that one might grab the wrong can, accidentally empty the green beans into the bowl at 12:33, freak out, pour the green beans into a Tupperware, wipe up the puce-colored water that spills on the counter, wash the bowl, open the can of chicken broth, and then realize it's 12:38, at which point one is well and truly fucked. Obviously eating is no longer an option, because it's one minute too late, so it is necessary to wait until 4:19, and then at 4:19 think, *Hey, I'm doing pretty well, I can forgo those green beans and by 6 p.m. be hunched in the garish orange bathroom stall at work*, where, at the end of your shift, pizza, soda, cotton candy, Skittles, and crackers are always floating in the toilet.

I was sitting home alone at lunch one day, having gained off-campus privileges, sipping chicken broth while watching *All My Children*. During the commercial break, dreading throwing up because my throat was sore, I suddenly paid attention to the ad for Dexatrim: a woman in a red bathing suit dancing about by a pool.

Take control of your body! went the TV jingle, while the bathing-suit lady pranced about and turned men's heads. *Take control of your life!*

I dumped the rest of my soup down the drain and headed for the pharmacy.

I stood in Sterling Drug, terrified of being spotted, nervous because the pharmacist's son Kyle had just become the Quiz Bowl math person. To him, I was surely a Good Kid, one of those straight-A's-and-piano-lessons types. I stood before the dizzying array of diet aids (one of which, a box of little chocolate squares that looked like it had been on the shelf forever, was actually called "Ayds"), trying to decide which would rocket me fastest to a life of green pants (or slacks, as it were) and glory. Finally I grabbed the Dexatrim, just as the commercial had instructed.

I paid for them with my head down, buying a pen and notebook at the same time so that maybe Kyle's dad would think I was picking up something for my mother while buying school supplies. When he greeted me warmly, I mumbled "Hi," then stuffed my purchases in my backpack and got out of there as fast as I could. In geometry, while the rest of the class talked about isosceles triangles, I pulled open the box, folded down the cardboard flaps, pulled out a shiny blister pack, and began what would become my love affair with speed, glorious speed!

Diet pills rapidly became the holy altar at which I prayed. Dexatrim all but eliminated my need to throw up, because if I took enough of it, I never needed to eat. Within a couple of weeks I was wearing the aforementioned slacks. And, except for the fact that I was always cold, always sick, always grouchy, barely speaking to my parents, had no friends, and still lived in Prairie Grove, things seemed pretty much perfect. Like I said: just as long as nothing was more important than food. This is how anorexia can save you. This is also how it can kill you. This is where living and dying become the same thing.

6

AT AGE THIRTY-SIX, *I finally went to Oaxaca, Mexico. Oaxaca City is a bizarre and beautiful place, with such traditions as* Noche de Rabanos, *the "Night of the Radishes," when the town square is taken over by intricate figurative sculptures carved from the red fleshy roots. But the Day of the Dead is its own glitter-spangled underworld celebration. On Halloween night, children in costumes ranging from skeletons to Ninja Turtles parade through the streets of a city alive with orange marigolds, mariachis, and creepily out-of-tune brass bands.*

Of course this sort of occasion calls for a tattoo, so I spent the evening in the studio of Dr. Lakra, whose assumed name is slang for both "filthy" and "scar." He inked a large, colorful sugar skull on my left calf, and when I returned to the U.S., Denise's appren-

tice Frank Ash tattooed words around it: "Take what you have learned here back to Krumville," Spalding Gray's reference to his own small town in Swimming to Cambodia. *Never forget the place you left, and when you return, tell stories of other lands.*

I was sixteen years old, five feet six inches tall, and 98 pounds when I first went to see Dr. Philip J. Thornton, Ph.D. It was an October afternoon when crepe-paper leaves danced down the stained-glass windows of the Episcopal church where he saw his patients.

I rattled through the door of his office.

I had taken to wearing a dozen rosaries and an antique stopwatch around my neck. I liked feeling them whack against my collarbones, and I liked that rosaries were a symbol of a religion other than Baptist (Catholicism being, like Judaism, one step away from Satan worship in the dominant theological paradigm). Just that morning I had sewn two darts in the waistband of the green pants. My hair, except for the long bangs that covered half my face, was chopped into two-inch spikes. This was an homage to my favorite book of the moment, Ernest Hemingway's *The Garden of Eden*, in which a man and woman, wanting to become indistinguishable from one another, get the same boyish haircut. It was also a rebellion against the prevalent hairstyle of the time, spiral perms topped with what I called "donut bangs." The other girls in Prairie Grove fanned out their curled bangs around a central circle of scalp, which was the donut hole, and the hair was the donut. In my failed attempts to fit in, I had flirted briefly with donut bangs, but I developed an intense aversion to waking up in the morning with my hair plastered to my face by a shellac of leftover Stiff Stuff.

In those days the hallways of my high school smelled like chicken sweat, Aqua Net, Forever Krystal (a *Dynasty*-themed perfume), and Hubba Bubba gum. On special days, these odors were commingled with the stench of formaldehyde wafting off the dissected fetal pigs in the biology lab. I sat in the back of the geometry classroom tapping out wild speed-fueled rhythms on my clavicles, grinding my teeth, and waiting to get the hell out.

I landed in Dr. Thornton's office shortly after my mother walked in on me changing clothes in my bedroom. I'd forgotten to lock the door. When she saw me, she yelped, then started crying.

After I left for school the next day, she read my diary. When I came home, she waved it at me and said, "You're going to see a doctor."

"I cannot BELIEVE you snooped on me!" I shrieked. "You had no right to do that!"

"I had EVERY right," my mother countered. "My child is starving herself. I don't even know who you are anymore. You come in here with dark circles under your eyes and you look like you're dying. You—"

"I do NOT look like I'm DYING," I huffed. "I look perfectly fine. I'm perfectly healthy. I'm making good grades. Leave me alone."

"You don't even go out with any of your friends anymore. You don't do any activities at school."

"Except pass," I said. "Except stay out of trouble and get

A's. Nobody at school likes me anyway. I don't know if you've noticed, but it's not like they're exactly beating down the door."

"Don't you get smart," said my dad, who had by then joined in the argument. The night ended, like so many others, with none of us speaking, Cameron hiding, and me falling asleep between the bed and the wall, undeserving of a mattress, holding back tears by clenching my teeth.

I moved further away from my family, and for that matter, from everyone I knew. I ran, I took Dexatrim, I drank pot after pot of black coffee, and I did my homework. I took Advanced Placement classes in history and English. I was on speed-fueled fire. I bought a membership to a gym in Fayetteville, went dutifully every day after school, and did my studying on the StairMaster. I had decided that my only hope of getting out of the hellhole that was my life and my hometown was to get into a foreign exchange student program as soon as possible.

The morning after my mother read my diary, she took me to the pediatrician, where I shivered in a blue paper gown before the man who, a decade and a half before, had laid his hands on my crowning head and pulled me out into the world. He asked me questions about various aspects of my so-called lifestyle. Did I exercise? Did I eat? Did I still menstruate?

He asked me if I threw up what I ate. I knew about bulimia, because I'd read everything the Prairie Grove, Farmington, and Fayetteville public libraries had to offer on the subject. So I used the word first: "I'm not bulimic." He looked at me the way a thousand other doctors were no doubt looking at a thousand other shivering fibbing girls in pediatric clinics at that very moment. I held his eye.

He said, "I think you might be."

I said nothing.

He went out into the hallway and my mother followed him in. He sat down at his desk and wrote *Dr. Philip J. Thornton* and a phone number on a prescription pad, and said, "I think you should call a friend of mine." And he handed me the name of the next person my mother would come to loathe and I would come to regard as my savior.

I still do.

The day I met Dr. Thornton I stood in front of my bathroom mirror admiring the tunnel of light between my thighs. I felt horribly excited and horribly insecure, so I tried on seven outfits, pulling them tightly around my body to see which ones made me look the most emaciated, the most genuinely anorexic (and therefore the most successfully eating-disordered). I did not want him to see me as bulimic, to picture me at the Skate Place with my fingers down my throat, tickling that little ledge of cartilage, *come hither*, coaxing my food back up. Rather, I wanted him to picture me as an ascetic, starving in a room that most definitely did not have rust-colored carpet and those little Styrofoam popcorn bits sprayed onto the ceiling.

Everything about him was worldly, starting with the fact that he wasn't Baptist. There were pictures on his packed bookshelves of him with his wife on a boat in some Italian canal, outside Harrods in London, and on a vibrant green hill in Ireland, and then there were shots of their well-educated children lined up outside colleges made of red brick.

"So, what brings you here?" he asked.

"My doctor made my parents bring me." I cringed at the admission of having parents. The last thing I wanted to do was spill my teenage guts to this guy with the beard and the little round glasses and the brown tweed jacket with the patches on the elbows—all of which, unfortunately, I found sexy. I tried not to find him sexy. I buried myself in my sweater with no small degree of embarrrassment.

"Do you like school?"

"I hate school."

"Is there anything about it you like?"

"English," I said. "But I hate when we have to read Shakespeare out loud and nobody understands that it's music. It hurts my ears when I have to hear it *reeeaallllly sloooow* with a hillbilly accent." My mother would have considered my comments conceited, and Zoe and Lula would have stopped speaking to me for at least a week; I'd referred to my peers as hillbillies, and thus felt that sharp familiar uprising of red behind my eyes, the one that signaled I was doing something I shouldn't but was going to do it anyway because it felt good. Which was something that sort of scared me. You'd think this would be one of the things I'd mention to a psychiatrist.

"You don't have much of an accent, do you?" he said.

"I try."

"Where would you rather be instead of Prairie Grove?"

"England." Why? Because Sting was from there, and I considered Sting the sexiest man alive.

"England is nice." He knew from personal experience. I didn't.

"I don't have an eating disorder," I said.

"I didn't say you did."

We stared.

"Do you have a boyfriend?" he asked.

"I did."

"What's his name?"

"Owen."

"Did you and Owen make love?" The room exploded. A hole opened up in the floor and the lower half of my body fell through. I pictured the two little naked homunculi from the "Love Is" notebook I had in third grade, the one I used when I played Harriet the Spy. *Make love.* Any phrase in the history of the known universe would have been better than that one. He suddenly transformed before my eyes into a sensitive seventies guy with a perm who taught people to paint barns and shrubbery, and then he was back and I was hot for him again.

"Yes," I squeaked. Once counted. One time we *made love.*

"Are you using any form of birth control?"

"I don't have periods," I said.

"Well, you should be menstruating if you're sixteen." *Menstruating. Menstruating and making love,* I thought, *that's me.*

"Sometimes I do," I said.

"How often?"

While everyone else in Prairie Grove was hanging out at the One-Stop Mart after school, sitting on the gates of their parked pickup trucks, drinking Cokes out of little glass bottles and listening to Def Leppard, I was at the Episcopal church answering questions about my period. Later that evening, when my classmates had taken off in their pickups to do donuts in somebody's cow pasture and spit Skoal juice out the windows, I sat at home shaking my foot seventeen thousand times (it just wouldn't stop, I just couldn't make it stop) and listening to the college radio station broadcasting from thirty miles away in an effort to learn what was actually cool in the real world, and thinking my favorite obsessive thought, *Maybe if I just get skinny enough Owen will like me again.*

"I dunno," I said. "I guess the last time was about two months ago."

"How long before that?"

"Can we talk about something else?"

"For now."

I kept him talking about something else for weeks. Mostly we talked about books. One day he gave me a copy of *Jonathan Livingston Seagull,* and I opened it up and smelled it.

"I do that too," he said. "Smell books."

"I go to the Dickson Street used book store and smell books for fun," I admitted.

"I'll have to try that sometime."

I suddenly felt the overwhelming urge to share another secret. "I lost my virginity to Oingo Boingo," I blurted randomly. "Like, not to the band itself, but that's what was playing."

"I don't know Oingo Boingo. What do they sound like?" he asked.

"Like horrible oompa bullshit," I replied, and he laughed, and I laughed, and I hugged the book, and I loved him.

Still, I lied, because the eating disorder remained my master, my primary allegiance. I lied to him all winter, mostly about food. One day I let it slip that I hadn't eaten since the previous morning, and he made me promise I'd stop for a cheeseburger after the session. Instead I ripped open a packet of saltines that had gone stale in my glove compartment. But I pretended they were a cheeseburger, so it counted a little. Two saltines were, after all, one-tenth of a cheeseburger. Which part of the cheeseburger would I have picked, had I actually eaten a tenth of one? I chewed my crackers in tiny squirrel bites and thought, *Cheese. Mayonnaise. Meat. Double cheese. Double meat. Four hundred all-beef patties, special sauce, lettuce, cheese, pickles, onions on two hundred sesame seed buns.*

I carried my secret around with me everywhere: I had a shrink. I was officially crazy. I went to see a psychiatrist after school. It made me feel special as opposed to just weird. I was certifiably *mad*, like Sylvia Plath or Anne Sexton; perhaps I would gas myself one day. I started to imagine that Phil could see everything—he took the place of Andy Warhol—and that he was watching me all the time. In the morning, I hooked my unnecessary bra around my xylophone ribs and imagined he could see my nonexistent breasts, and my face flushed hot. I went to school, popped my five Dexatrim—he looked away during that part, but he followed me to geometry, where I stared out the window and sang Police songs in my head. I began to wonder whether everything I did was pathological. I asked him one day if I could read the *Diagnostic and Statistical Manual,* the "DSM," as he called it, the leather-bound tome of things that could be wrong with people.

"You just want to smell the book," he said.

In my memory, every time Phil gave me a book, the hand-off looked sort of like the ceiling of the Sistine Chapel. That's how important and momentous it felt. I began to realize that people can be healed by telling each other stories.

Of course, this is overly romantic; storytelling didn't avert the rapidly increasing hypomanic episodes, nor did it save me from running a sobering gauntlet of medications for over a decade. But having a grown-up tell me with obvious passion and conviction that books were important, I mean *really* important and not just reach-this-degree-of-literacy-and-pass-this-test important, blew something open inside me, something that had been waiting to be blown open. I gave him a copy of *Interview with the Vampire* and he read it, and this fueled our conversations that first year. We found each other in the pages.

Out of nowhere, Owen began to call me occasionally and continued to break my heart. I prayed to a God in whom I no longer believed: *Please please please bring him back to me I'll eat less I promise.* And I ate less, and sure enough, a month later, I came home to a hand-folded note in my mailbox. "We had a good thing and I blew it," it said. That night we reconciled, hotly, in his Mazda RX-7 in the parking lot behind the church, though we did not *make love* because the seat didn't go back far enough.

I couldn't tell my parents we were back together. They hated him, and rightly so—I'd wept and wailed and gnashed my teeth over him for so long that they just simply couldn't take it anymore. The grand high drama of my adolescent love life, combined with the grand high drama of my adolescent self-destruction, was the reason they were paying Dr. Thornton the big bucks to talk to me. But with Owen's love, Dr. Thornton's positive influence decreased somewhat—I was complete, I was whole, as long as Owen gave me any attention at all. I did not need to be anything more than his girlfriend (and skinny). I sank into a malnourished calm, a path-of-least-resistance serenity, in which I viewed starvation as voodoo, my primary means of making him behave the way I wanted him to. I snuggled my tiny broken body into Owen's muscular arms whenever possible, and I tried to ignore the people who said they saw him with Lana Hailey in the parking lot at the bonfire and that all you could see was her bare feet pressed against his windshield. I had discovered the great secret: Stop eating until nothing matters anymore. Stop eating until you have no more energy to fight. Stop eating until you're eighteen and you can get out of Prairie Grove.

Phil called it a "moratorium."

"What's that?" I asked, from the island of the couch, wrapped in two sweaters, my bones like glass bells.

"It means you're putting everything on hold until you can deal with it."

"I can deal with it."

We stared some more. My heart leapt unexpectedly across the room at him, *please save me*, then ricocheted back into my sternum.

"It's not doing us any good to talk about weight. We have to find the thing that's going to give you a reason to stay alive." I opened my mouth. He said, "Besides Owen. You want to leave Prairie Grove, right? You want to get out? Okay. Let's make a plan for you to do that. You're too important to starve to death."

I crumbled. I cried. I tried to find the right words—*I don't mean to be so stupid, I'll eat, I won't eat, I'll do whatever you want me to do*—but the words didn't come. Finally I wiped my eyes and said, "What I really want is to be an exchange student in Europe."

"Fine, then," he said. "That's a perfectly reasonable goal. But you have to be healthy to do it, so let's get you healthy again."

That spring, tears came more and more frequently. I buried my face in his couch and I realized, for the first time but certainly not the last, that apologizing could be a weapon. You can apologize until people think you're crazy. Your whole body can become an apology. You're not skinny enough or smart enough or pretty enough or talented enough or sexy enough or popular enough or sophisticated enough or tall enough or short enough or blond enough or like the last girl enough and you're sorry, you're sorry, you're sorry. When you realize that not only are you not making people love you, you're actively making them hate you, you think, *Oh, they still hate me, I knew it all along, but surely five more pounds or this color hair dye or winning this award or making my 2,500-word papers exactly 2,500 words, surely* that *will make them love me. Of course, they hate me now, I'm not enough yet, but I will be. I promise.* Anorexia is good at making you think your own thoughts are those of other people.

At Phil's insistence, and despite my mother's opposition to travel of any sort, I went away in the summer of 1988 to

Arkansas Governor's School. It was a six-week liberal arts camp at Hendrix College, started by Bill Clinton, who had breakfast with us the first day. I remember sitting and watching him eat a lot of biscuits. Today, in New York City, when people say, "Arkansas? Do you know Bill Clinton?" I answer, "Yeah, I once watched him eat a lot of biscuits." If I'm feeling saucy, I say I blew him.

While he was eating the biscuits? they ask.

In order to get into Governor's School, you had to be one of the "hundred most gifted and talented high school students in Arkansas," which apparently someone decided I was. I had struggled over the application in Phil's office, while steadily gaining just enough weight that he, my pediatrician, and my parents would let me go.

"I'm very proud of you," said Phil on the day I brought in the acceptance letter. "You're putting yourself in harm's way, just like we talked about. You'll just do it bigger and better every time from here on out." *Harm's way* was one of Phil's favorite expressions—he often told me it was where I needed to put myself, to teach myself that I could do it in a controlled manner and survive. His words were prophetic, foretelling not only the achievements but the manias and the suicide attempts to come. Bigger and better every time, yup. I would become a master of the melodramatic spectacle. I would take everything positive out of the idea of "harm's way," focusing only on the harm.

Hendrix College is in a little town called Conway, half an hour from Little Rock, where you can buy a T-shirt celebrating the fact that Conway is between two towns called Toad

Suck and Pickles Gap. In the town square, there's a big green toad in a big red circle, and the toad is wearing overalls and a straw hat and chewing a blade of grass, and around the circle it says TOAD SUCK DAZE, the name of a local festival. I decided these embarrassing facts would not keep me from learning something about literature during my time in Conway, and learn about literature I did. Governor's School would be one of the best things to ever happen to me.

My parents moved me into my dorm room on a swelter-ing June day, my mother and I barely speaking. She was mad at me for wearing only one earring, which she thought I was doing in an attempt to get attention for being weird. She told me I needed to stop trying to look like Denise Huxtable and tone it down a bit if I was ever going to have any friends; I told her she was being ridiculous. She wished me a tight-lipped goodbye, and I sat on the foot of my bed with my feet on my suitcase and got to know my roommate Julie, who had come to Governor's School to study drama, as she attempted to hang a *Les Misérables* beach towel on the wall with Sticky Tack. She wore a *Les Misérables* T-shirt and had a *Les Misérables* pillow-case. Her parents took her to New York City, she said, so she could see the Broadway show for her birthday. She had among her tape cassettes two versions of the cast recording.

"I'll have to play you 'Master of the House,'" she said, "It's so good. You'll sing it for days."

At one point she punctuated her chatter with, "My shrink's really glad I'm here," and I was shocked, but then realized she was from Little Rock, where people were rich and sophis-ticated and probably everybody had a therapist, just like in

Woody Allen movies. When Julie told me she was Jewish—the first Jew I'd ever met, which meant I found her very exotic— I knew I'd finally found my way into an environment where people were truly sophisticated. I said, "Yeah, *my* shrink's glad too."

She brightened, ready to hear the lowdown on someone else's craziness. "Why are you seeing a shrink?"

"Because I'm anorexic and bulimic," I said, having decided that here, if anyone asked, I would admit it. I had started to think I might spend the summer writing a story about it to send to *Seventeen* magazine.

"Eww, you puke?" she said with glee.

"Yup."

"Every day?"

"Not anymore." It was true. I had gotten better, a little bit, tenuously.

"I'm just dyslexic," she said. "And hyper. I take Ritalin. Just about everybody I know takes Ritalin. Do you?"

"No."

"Most of us just sell it to the cheerleaders as diet pills," she laughed, pushing her glasses farther up her nose and wiping her brow with her forearm. The towel, at last, was secured to the wall with so much Sticky Tack the little urchin's face looked all lumpy, like on top of everything else she had to endure, she'd come down with the mumps.

"Well, I take diet pills already," I said.

"You *do*? That's so bad for you."

"Yeah," I said, "but not as many as I used to. I used to take a lot."

"Moderation is a good thing," she mused. "Excess is so Edie Sedgwick."

I was in a place where people knew who Edie Sedgwick was! My heart swam. I was with the cool kids, finally, at last. For the next six weeks, I could be anybody I wanted. I decided that I would wholeheartedly embrace my one-earringed weirdness and become an eccentric literary genius.

I quickly settled into the whirlwind, mind-blowing routine of Areas I, II, and III. Area I was your primary subject. You had two Area I classes a day; mine were creative writing and short stories. Then you had Area II, which was basically a philosophy class, where you and twenty other kids from different majors talked about the existence of God, the pros and cons of torture, and the idea of utopian society. Area III was the touchy-feely one, where you "processed" everything that was happening to you. When asked by our hippie watercolor-painter teacher to write on notecards what we expected from Area III, I made the embarrassing mistake of writing in smudgy erasable pen that I expected it to be a little like the sessions I was missing with my shrink. She pulled me aside to talk to me; I reiterated the eating disorder story. I must admit I liked the cachet it gave me. Eccentric *troubled* literary genius: I relished the extra adjective.

I presented myself as a Very Serious Author, wearing the hell out of my F. Scott Fitzgerald T-shirt. Because I was obsessed at the time, having read that she was Sting's favorite author, I started the Church of Anne Rice, which meant I wrote *Interview with the Vampire* with red and black Sharpies on a lot of people's jeans. I went to a costume party as Gabrielle de Lioncourt, Lestat's mom, who wore black spandex pants according to my interpretation. At night I danced with the visual arts kids to the Smiths on the roof of the library, and I loved them because they all dressed in black and had bangs that obscured one of their eyes. If they were wearing more than one earring, their asymmetrical haircuts didn't show it. Swaying beneath the moon, surrounded by kids who looked like Deiter from *Sprockets*, I felt gloriously at home.

We watched films; I became a film freak at Governor's School. I learned about Leni Riefenstahl and Frederick Wiseman, and took in *Dr. Strangelove* and *Brazil* and *My Life as a Dog*, as well as Pink Floyd's *The Wall* (which, embarrassingly enough, was probably the one that affected me the most; perhaps it is a not a film meant to be seen sober). Exhausted, my brain overloaded with stimuli, I nodded off at my desk after writing in my journal: *Maybe Pink shaves his eyebrows because he wants to mutilate himself out of mourning for his friends in the hamburger grinder.*

We read *Kaspar* and *Offending the Audience* by Peter Handke. A man who freely admitted to being an atheist came in and gave a lecture on subliminal advertising to all the Area II classes. I learned that they stamp SEX into Ritz crackers and put pictures of screaming faces in the ice cubes in liquor ads because this will remind alcoholics of withdrawal and they'll keep drinking. I gleefully turned into a Socialist conspiracy theorist with a penchant for German Expressionism. I wrote stories about girls who were incarcerated for killing their parents. Then I discovered Flannery O'Connor, fell madly and passionately in love, and declared Anne Rice a hack.

The moratorium, as Phil called it, was over. One day, in the cafeteria, my new friend Nicki and I picked up a package of NoSalt, the salt substitute, and because we had been primed for weeks to rage against the machine, we taped NoSalt packets to pieces of posterboard and marched around protesting. Our protest consisted primarily of running up to people, ripping open a packet, throwing it at them, screaming *"No Salt!"* and running away. Given permission to question anything, I questioned everything. I told Julie that actually I was not such a big fan of "Master of the House." I decided I definitely, for sure, did not believe in God. I was one step closer to grown-up. Officially freed from Christianity, the eating disorder fading in the presence of stronger passions, I was almost happy.

So why, then, did I buy the Dexatrim? Maybe because when I walked into the student bookstore one day with a headache and a plan to buy some aspirin, the Dexatrim was *right fucking there. Hmm,* I thought, *college girls take it.* Julie had found the box I'd brought with me to camp and thrown it away, and I'd been okay without it. I knew I didn't need it. But in an instant I forgot about the aspirin and got the Dexatrim instead, easy as that. Seeing it on the shelf in the Hendrix bookstore made it acceptable, normal, no big deal. Because I didn't want to be seen buying just diet pills, I picked up an M. C. Escher poster. This seemed like a well-rounded collegiate bookstore purchase.

In my room my fingers tripped over the box in my rush to open it: *My love, I have missed you.* It had only been a month, but a month was a long time. How many pills could I have taken in that time? Ten a day, that's what, three hundred?

Three thousand? Something like that? This box had only thirty. I could take the whole thing.

As I popped open the blister packs, I thought of all the other things I could be doing: writing a story, reading a story, dancing with the artfags, protesting something. Seeing a movie, having a discussion, walking through the library smelling books. Coffee in the student center, cigarettes on the fire escape, anything, the world was my oyster. Right? I mean, that's what they tell you. They tell you you can do anything, they tell you your brain is important, they tell you you're one of the most gifted and talented blah blah blah blah blah, and then they say, *Look, here between the books, doncha wanna be skinny, little girl?*

College girls did it. It had to be okay. I took Julie's plastic *Les Misérables* tumbler to the bathroom, turned on the tap, and served myself what was for all intents and purposes a bucket of water. A 44-ounce *Les Mis* commemorative beverage was just what the occasion called for.

This is what people with eating disorders do: we drink lots of liquids. After all, if you chug a half gallon of water before dinner, you'll be fine with just carrots and an apple. If you fool yourself with 64 ounces of Diet Coke, you won't need actual nutrients. If you take a sip before each bite during a binge, and slam a liter bottle of whatever just before purging, it comes up easier. I had asked for a chance to go away and use my mind and I had gotten it, and yet there I was sitting on the floor eating pills. Thinking: *I could kill myself. I could do it. Right here, this could be it, my mother wouldn't be the one to find me.* I wasn't scared.

I decided to take a shower, thinking that maybe the hot water would increase my circulation and get the diet pills into my system faster so I could sit at dinner being all impressive with my ability not to eat. I washed my left arm, then my right. As I scrubbed my face, I noticed there was suddenly a strobe light in the shower. I could see every individual drop coming from the showerhead. It occurred to me, with a sudden manic flash, that showers and busy signals were EXACTLY THE SAME THING! Why had I never realized this before? Everything began to go *reallyreallyfast,* my vision narrowed to a tiny white dot, and I opened my mouth to scream but the water poured in and my voice was drowned.

My head hit the wall in a broken line like the water droplets: *thump thump thump.* I covered the drain with my body and the shower turned into a little swimming pool. I lay there for a while thinking, *Something's not right here,* and then it occurred to me that the thing to do would be to *stand up. STAND UP! STAND UUUUPPPPP!!!*

I stood up. Or at least halfway. I crawled. Left the shower running, crawled to the bathroom door, somehow got the door open, crawled down the hall. Everyone else was at dinner. I could have been eating dinner. Instead, I was having *THE TIME OF MY LIFE!* I was thin and popular and in demand! The glamour was nonstop!

I left a trail of soap suds in the hallway of the dorm, immensely grateful that there was nobody around to see me squelching along, unable to dry myself or walk without hanging onto the wall. The towel I had used to wrap myself was soaking wet, so when I got back to my room, I pulled myself up on the doorknob, opened the door, thought, *OH, I REALLY NEED A DRY TOWEL*, and ripped the *Les Mis* beach towel down on top of myself.

By the time Julie returned to the room, I had managed to dress myself in shorts and an old sweatshirt and lay sprawled on the red beanbag chair. She yelped when she saw her towel across the foot of my bed and little Sticky Tack pellets all over the room. I said nothing, just let her eyes travel to the empty Dexatrim blister-packs on my desk and her half-full tumbler beside them.

"I'm glad you're all right," she said. "Incidentally, I'm never speaking to you again."

And she didn't. She sat at her desk reading a script all evening, and then she went to bed. I remained in the beanbag until she fell asleep, listening to my Walkman, afraid to move lest my head fall apart. I sat tapping my foot to the music all night, still too wired to sleep, silently chanting: *Sorry, sorry, sorry, sorry, I'm sorry. Sorry about your towel, towel, towel, towel, towel.* My teeth clanged against each other, the echoes bouncing off my guts. I stayed like that until it turned blue outside, then white. With Julie still asleep, I crept to the bathroom, brushed my teeth, and took another shower, and then crawled out onto the fire escape to look for half-smoked cigarettes. Found some, smoked them. I had an overwhelming urge to call Phil, which I could do at nine o'clock, as soon as he got to his office. I managed to wait it out.

His secretary's voice, then his—beautiful, soothing. I told him I needed help, that it had all been going well but yesterday it went to shit.

"I'm sorry," I said. "I fucked up. I don't know what's wrong with me."

"Sometimes," he said, "when you put yourself in harm's way, you get harmed. In your case, you harmed yourself. Interesting development."

I laughed, felt guilty for laughing. But he chuckled with me, and I was so grateful for his irreverence I wanted to leap through the phone and hug him.

"That doesn't mean, of course, that it's okay. Do you need medical attention?"

"No," I said, "I'm alive."

"Good," he said. "Stay that way. Absolutely no more diet pills, you have things to learn and I'd be very disappointed if you died before you learned them."

"Me too." For the first time, I really meant it. Knowing there was someone out there who actively wanted me to stay alive because he thought I had something to offer was such a novel concept, I couldn't let him down.

"It's like this," he said. "Your job right now is to try, and fail, and try again. The trying is more important than the failing. Eventually you won't be afraid of either."

"I'm tired of starving," I said.

"Good," he said. "Cut it out."

And it seemed almost, almost that easy.

I thought about how, in just a few weeks, I would be a senior in high school. After that I could leave. I had less than three hundred and sixty-five days left in Prairie Grove, and then I never had to see it again if I didn't want to. But first, I had to pass Algebra II. I had to fill out college applications. I had to go back to the snack bar at the Skate Place and make the cotton candy. But most of all, I had to be an exchange student. I had to leave the country and prove to myself I could.

I would.

As soon as I returned to Prairie Grove, I marched myself into the school counselor's office and requested an application for a study-abroad program. She found one called the American Institute for Foreign Study, and I applied to Richmond College, an international university in London. While waiting for the acceptance letter, which came several weeks later, I found a higher-paying job at a clothing store in the mall in order to save up the $2,500 tuition. When I told Phil, he hooted with joy and applauded.

More than any other person in my life, I have him to thank for setting me on the path to becoming the person I am today. For the first time, I chose a savior and actually found him worthy of the title.

Unfortunately, I would experience my first manic episode in London.

7

WORDS I'VE SEEN *written on people's bodies:*

1. *Taz Kwon Do*
2. *#1 Ozzy Fan*
3. *POT*
4. *Hecho en México*
5. *Poor Impulse Control*
6. *MARY (across entire chest)*
7. *Rightous [sic] (across the back of the right hand)*

Words written on my body:

1. *Eureka*
2. *This Long, Thin Line*

3. *This Electrical Machine*

4. *Love*

5. *Hate*

6. *Jolt*

7. *Wait! Don't answer it!*

8. *Wildcat Frenchie*

9. *Harm's Way*

10. *When disturbed by disturbing thoughts, think of the opposite*

11. *Take what you have learned here back to Krumville*

I am wordy.

Summer 1989. There was a plane and I was on it.

It was the day after my high school graduation, where I sat in the gym, sweltering; it was raining and muggy outside, and the bleachers were packed with people. I felt stupid in my hat. The pregnant valedictorian sang a song about how friends are friends forever if the Lord's the Lord of them, reminding me how glad I was that the Lord was not the Lord of me, and that I therefore was under no further obligation to pretend these people were my friends. I threw my hat in the air and was out the door before it landed. Others scuffled to retrieve their tassels to hang from their rearview mirrors. I tugged my gown off on the way to the car and chucked it in the trash. Marcus Hawley got in his car and hung his tassel from his mirror. I peeled off my parking permit.

And then there was this plane and it was going to London and I was inside and looking out the window, watching home get smaller. It was my first plane ride, and despite my mother's protests, despite all the reasons she had given me why this was a bad idea, I was going to England by myself to study literature for the summer.

My dad drove me to the Dallas airport and slipped me five hundred bucks at the gate. "Don't tell your mother," he said. I put the money in my pocket and clutched my ticket in my hand and got on the plane and went up in the air and then there I was, finally, flying.

The first time I heard music split apart, I was on the plane. I was listening to Prince on my headphones when all of a sudden I could hear all the instruments solo, but at the same time. Like when you say, *I'm just going to listen to the guitar,* so you shut your ears to everything else and just hear the guitar. Well, I did that with all the instruments at once, and when it happened, it gives me goose bumps. And not in a good way.

There was red on the wing of the plane, and when the music split, the red amplified itself times a million and burned my eyes. Everything around me liquefied—the air, my seat, my hands, the little girl beside me eating taffy, she was water, everything was wet.

And then just as quickly, it stopped. I tried to put it out of my mind, even though I knew my mind was where it lived, and I was terrified. By the end of the summer, I would find that occasionally everybody sounded like they were talking into fans, and I had to wait a few seconds for their words to settle. The voices were chopped apart, then they put themselves back together. I would look around me as the sound shifted back into place and wonder if anyone else had noticed. It made me sweat. I hated how it made me sweat.

It also made me feel instantaneously exhausted, which I now assume was due to sleep deprivation. The splitting of sound was my body's signal that it would indeed eventually pass out, whether I wanted to or not. No matter how enervated one feels, no matter how much one's environment, biochemistry, and fucked-up circadian rhythms have led one to believe that one has superpowers, one will eventually give way to sleep. When I fell asleep on the plane that day, dreams of Prairie Grove intertwined themselves with a London I'd seen only in pictures.

Upon waking, I decided to take advantage of the fact that I could drink on the plane, because it was British Air and in England the legal drinking age was eighteen. I didn't particularly like alcohol, but then, I'd only had wine coolers. So I ordered cognac. I didn't know what cognac was, exactly, but it was the most sophisticated drink I could think of. By the time we landed, I'd had four of them, mixed with Sprite. I had never been drunk before. I hadn't even made it to England yet and already I'd had a new life experience. My decision to repeat that experience with some regularity over the next few months no doubt exacerbated the craziness, but it would be a long time before I would figure out there was a connection between alcohol, drugs, and mood swings. In some ways, I am a slow learner.

I somehow managed to navigate Gatwick Airport, took a ride over cobblestone streets in a little black taxi, and puked when I get out. I overpaid the taxi driver exorbitantly because I was too drunk and nervous to figure out the money. Anything that could indicate to anyone that I was a hillbilly foreigner was verboten. According to the Institute for Foreign Study pamphlets sent shortly before my arrival, it was best to travel with only a backpack. I had done so, but stuffed three pairs of shoes into said backpack, because I was afraid Prairie Grove shoes might get laughed at over there.

My dorm was in Kensington, a very fancy neighborhood— or, as my cabdriver called it, "posh." I went inside, talked to a curly-haired girl behind a desk whose name tag said *Nicki Sawicki*, got a key, found the room, opened the door, and saw a large black man and a large black woman having sex. He jumped off of her. They laughed, like it happened every day. He apologized in a British accent.

Nauseous and blurred, I told her I thought I was her roommate. She threw on a robe and introduced herself, said she was from Gambia, which was in Africa, and told me her very long African name but said, "Call me Lali."

"Okay, Lali," I said. "I'm Stacy. I need a nap."

I passed out on the bed on which they were not fucking and dreamt I was being abducted by aliens. They came through the window and carried me off on a beam of light. I floated over London and looked down, disoriented because there were no Baptist churches. When I woke, I had a vague sensation that the aliens had been feeding me blueberry pie.

Pie: I was hungry. It was dark. I went outside, walked a block, found a café, and bought myself a scandalously overpriced ham sandwich—by which I mean bread and ham and that's it. I thought, *None of that fancy condiment shit for the British*, and I giggled out loud, too loud, all by myself. Was I really there? As I sat in the window gnawing on the hard bread, the first baguette I'd ever had, I saw two women walk by with big black antique strollers I knew they called prams, and we did not have prams in Arkansas, and I was indeed somewhere else and I was elated. I'd done it. I'd gotten out. Furthermore, I could eat all the ham sandwiches I wanted and pay six pounds each for them, because really this was just play money anyway. It had colors. One was red, bright red. Or at least that's how I remember it.

When I finished the sandwich, I wandered through the streets until I found a jazz club. It was called the Harlem Hotcha, and they had a drink called the Harlem Blues, which comprised, by my estimation, every kind of liquor ever made, plus blue food coloring. Because I could, I ordered one. I also ordered chocolate ice cream, which came with chocolate syrup and a crunchy waffle fin. I learned that if you drank the entire blue thing, you get to keep the glass, and the glass was cool, so I drank the entire blue thing. In twenty-four hours, I'd had more liquor than I'd ever had in all my life combined. I ate all the ice cream and dug on the upright bass, which I had never actually seen anybody play in real life (insert Journey: *Just a small-town girl* . . .). I do not remember going home, but in the morning, the glass was on my desk, complete with a soggy paper umbrella.

Lali was dressing herself in a white T-shirt with no bra, her massive ebony breasts pendulous, to her waist. The previous day I'd awakened in my room in Arkansas, and the walls were painted peach and there was a Bible on the bookshelf, and today I was looking at the first dark brown breasts I'd ever seen. Also, for the second time, I was hungover.

"Good morning," Lali sang. "Sorry about yesterday." She hurried out the door on her way to class. When she left, I snooped through her desk and found a Ziploc bag of used condoms, tied off at the ends, full of what I assumed was the semen of the young gentleman atop her the day before. I didn't want to know. I was a stranger in a strange land, and, there alone, I was rapidly deconstructing. The *world* was deconstructing. Nothing was as it should be. I was terrified.

I showered down the hall in a stall with no curtain and the smell of my Vidal Sassoon shampoo made me gag. Puking voluntarily is one thing, but puking involuntarily sucks. If I'm going to vomit, I want to have control over it. I decided I would never drink again, a promise I would break in short order.

I went to my first class, the first college class I'd ever taken, and sat next to a blond girl who wore no shoes. Her bare feet were dirty, like she'd walked all over the city. Were these things real? I remember them as real, but now, twenty years later, they seem impossible and absurd. Still, this is what my brain tells me, what my senses led me to believe, and though my memories are those of the mad, they are mine.

After class, I followed my professor—whose name was, in a strange twist of fate, Dr. Southern—to the cafeteria. Because I wanted to look smart, I asked him if he liked Anthony Burgess, who wrote *A Clockwork Orange*. I was proud of myself for having subsequently plowed through a wordy doorstop called *Enderby*, and wanted to find a way to impress him with this fact. He said, "Oh, my dear, some writers write as if they've memorized dictionaries. Anthony Burgess *swallowed* one." Conversation over, we ate potato soup, the first of many potato-based foodstuffs I would consume in England. Potatoes, I would find, could generally be counted on not to contain kidneys or other frightening meat. Plus, they made me sleepy. That night I fell asleep staring out my window, and in my dream I was still staring out the window, and then the aliens in their spaceship were there. Somehow this dream made me even more tired. I did not want these aliens.

I began, over the next week, to sleep less and less. Sleep seemed increasingly irrelevant in London. There was so much to do! There were so many places with bright lights where they were happy to take your money! In a whirlwind of impulsiveness for which the borderline and bipolar are known, I purchased a pair of expensive silk pants at Kensington Market, because they were purple paisley and purple and paisley both started with *p*, as did Prince, who wore purple paisley. Good things came in threes; it seemed prophetic that I should find these pants and wear them all summer. Big full pantaloons, another word that started with *p* (therefore interfering with the rule of threes and making me quite uncomfortable, as though I would bring misfortune upon myself for having calculated incorrectly), made my legs sweat, so I cut them off at the knees—or, at least, that was the intention. One side came out significantly higher than the other, like one leg ended at the knee and one mid-thigh. They started to unravel. I began to obsessively pluck all the shiny gold and silver threads and drop one every three blocks. Step, step, step, step, step, hold, drop. I walked to class and through Hyde Park that way. That bass from the jazz club had been stuck in my head for days, and I had to match the rhythm to the dropping of the threads. Five notes repeated themselves over and over for a week— something that still happens to me now, despite medication, and still drives me nuts—and I had to try to sing them in my throat while I walked (this, too, still happens, and is pro- foundly uncomfortable). I had to feel the notes in there but not actually let them out, because then I'd really be a crazy person. As long as I didn't vocalize, I figured I was still holding on, still just barely sane, but there was one note I couldn't hit. My throat kept opening and I could feel the note down in my chest, and the way my vocal cords were pushing down made it feel like the music was literally hurting my heart.

The bright spot in that first week in London was that I met a lifelong friend in the dorm. Her name was Yael, and she was from Los Angeles. Her father was a psychiatrist, and, as such, she had lots of money. Yael was only the second Jewish person I had ever met, after my Governor's School roommate Julie. She was so Jewish she was actually born in Israel, and it made me feel very worldly to know her.

I also met a guy named Geoff and started making out with him every night. I wasn't really attracted to him, and we never actually had sex, but we did things I had never done, like when he poured Evian water on my breasts and licked it off. Yael's room was next door to Geoff's, and she came over one night asking if he had her Jane's Addiction tape. She looked at me, disheveled on the bed, accurately assessed my discomfort with Geoff (though, again with the impulsivity, I couldn't stop making out with him) and said, "I'm out of tampons. Do you have any? Let's go to your room." As we climbed the stairs, she said, "You don't need to fuck some idiot for excitement. I want to go to Spain this weekend. You're coming with me." Just like that, my instant advocate and friend. I was profoundly honored and grateful.

"How will we get there?"

"There's a student travel agency that sells round-trip plane tickets to Barcelona for ninety-nine pounds," she says, "We're totally going."

What I knew about Barcelona was that they pronounced it *Barthelona*. When I learned that in high school it got stuck in my head all day. Swept up in Yael's confidence, authority, and desire to be my friend, I followed her to the travel agent's that afternoon and we bought tickets. Two-fifths of my money was gone, and I still had over two months left in Europe. No matter, I'd just spend less now, really.

That night the aliens came again. There was a new book out called *Communion* by Whitley Streiber, which I remembered because I liked the sound of his name, and I liked how it had four syllables that go DUH-duh DUH-duh. It was about aliens who looked just like the aliens in my dreams. In that night's incarnation of the dream, the spaceship went back and forth past the window a few times, then stopped, and one of the aliens looked out the window and gave me a little army salute. It winked at me and clicked its tongue, as if to say, *Here's lookin' at you.* It shot a beam of light into my room and sucked me into the spaceship, where we once again ate blueberry pie.

Every day after I had the alien dreams I would see this book

Communion. It was like it found me and snuck up on me. I'd just be walking along, and I'd just happen to turn my head, and there in the window of a bookstore would be *Communion.* Or I'd be walking through Hyde Park and just happen to see someone reading it on a bench. Of all the benches I could have turned my head and looked at, it was always the one where there *just happened* to be someone sitting and reading *Communion.* I was certain someone from another dimension was trying to tell me something—another blurring of what was in the world and what was in my head. I told myself, *It's just coincidence,* and something in me responded *No it's not.* I didn't know this other voice living inside me, but I knew it was an intruder, and I didn't like it.

On top of all this, Dustin Hoffman was in the stage version of some Shakespeare play and living in my neighborhood. Geoff said he jogged in Hyde Park a lot. Sure enough, I began to see him everywhere, or at least to think I did, and I thought that was a sign from the aliens as well. Saying what, I don't know; my thoughts were going too fast to figure that out. I thought I saw him in several different locations reading *Communion.* I knew that surely this could not be real, but my brain had never gone that fast. I knew things I had never learned. It is easy to believe you're superhuman when you suddenly become extraordinarily facile with words and numbers, and when you receive messages everywhere you go.

That weekend, I went for my second ride on an airplane, this time with Yael. The sound of the propellers did that breaking-apart thing—and from here on, my memories of Europe are mostly colors and sounds and lights on the back of my eyelids. Barcelona was, as I recall, mostly bright green. It was a bright green city. They liked the bright green there, in Barcelona, a lot.

Snapshots: there were transvestite hookers outside our hostel. Inside, the lights were on timers. The bathroom was at the end of the hall, and you had to push a button and run for it to get there in your allotted portion of light. The floor was covered with cockroaches as big as a human hand. Yael said, "Fuck that," and peed in the sink. She slept wearing a T-shirt but no underwear, which meant that I saw a lot of her vagina. One morning she slashed the big vein in her ankle by accident, shaving, and when I opened my eyes her bloody foot was on my pillow, and she said, "Is this an important vein?" and I looked up and saw her vagina.

I wandered through Barcelona for four days, and sometimes Yael was there, and sometimes not. At some point I fell asleep on a beach, the first sleep I'd had since we got there. I woke up covered in sand, wearing a bikini, with a vague memory of meeting some Swedish guys in the plaza and eating chocolate ice cream and agreeing to go with them to a town called Blanes. We were in a car, a sports car, a convertible. How long did it take? An hour, two? Where were the Swedes now? Where was Yael? Were we in Blanes? Where did Barcelona go? I laughed. As if cities could just disappear! You'd really have to be crazy to think that.

Although I don't believe in a God with nothing better to do than watch out for us idiots, something certainly kept me from dying in Spain. I am, on reflection, amazed I survived. I really have no memory of getting from place to place, or of the passage of time. I know I was in Spain for four days, because I have the boarding passes in a scrapbook, but in my mind the trip is both a tiny speck and an epic journey. (Both borderline personality and bipolar disorder have as a significant feature the occasional fluxy sense of time, another reason I strongly believe they belong on the same continuum.) It seems as though I was in Blanes for a long while, but in reality it couldn't have been more than a day.

I decided the reason my thoughts had started going so fast as soon as I got away from home was that I was making up for lost time. I was educating myself, compensating for eighteen years of not being educated in the way I would have liked. Here, I would not be called a snob for wanting more. I was not a snob, I was a genius, and my thoughts were finally moving at genius speed.

I wasn't crazy, I was just in a hurry. *A hurry flurry with cream cheese and squirrel on top,* shouted the part of me that suddenly delighted in ridiculous strings of words. I laughed. I was a badass. I was, in fact, such a badass I was sleeping topless in a paisley diaper on some beach that might or might not still be in—what was that country? Spain? Ah Spain, yes—Barcelona, Spain, the green place, and now Blanes, which appeared to have quite a cliff-diving scene. People flung themselves off steep rocks, doing flips in the air, and it was suddenly and wholly the most beautiful thing I'd ever seen. It seemed that the aliens must surely have brought me there to jump off a cliff. If everyone else was doing it . . .

Yes. Why yes, it seemed that I would.

I headed for the cliffs. I had to climb up to where the divers were, just had to. I was compelled in a way I'd never been before in my life. In that moment, I was certain the whole entire reason I was put on earth was to go up that cliff and fling myself from it. At the top there would no doubt be an epiphany, I was certain of it. *Epiphany is an awesome word that would make a good middle name*, shouted the clever thing inside me. And because "Blanes" and "Barcelona" had five letters in common, a fact I realized in a flash, I knew I was doing the right thing. It was a sign, like all the other signs bombarding me. So many signs. They had to mean something.

The rocks were slippery. They felt like eels beneath my feet. The tactile sensation was so real I began to think the rocks might actually be made of eels, and then I had to hop around trying to see how much of my weight I could balance on how little of my foot. Eel feet, ew. I had a sudden, violent thought of killing eels and I walked, and it was so vivid I almost started crying out of pity for every animal that had ever been killed. But just as quickly the sensation passed, and finally I got to the place where the divers were, and they were all boys, and they were glad to see me, as boys usually are when you're a girl in a bikini. I told them in what I thought was some universal language that I wanted to jump, and because I was nervous I tugged on my earlobe and realized I'd lost one of my silver earrings. The little dangling silver balls, my favorites. I was used to how they felt and the way they kept my head balanced, and now my head would be unbalanced, and again I almost cried for my lonely little earring lost at sea. I freaked out and remembered, with sudden clarity, that I was deathly afraid of heights.

I tried to run but the boys put their hands on me. Lots and lots of hands, trying to keep me from slipping down the side of Eel Mountain. They said what I believe amounted to "Jump, jump," as if this would somehow be preferable to the situation I was in right now.

I got down. How? Did I jump? I have no memory. If I did jump, if I did actually manage to cliff-dive at some juncture, I would like to know about it. C'est la vie.

In the next snapshot I was on a boat, having met two more Spanish guys. They were fishermen, and they spoke no English. But we were somehow communicating, and we were laughing, and there were fish in nets, silvery-red, and they were flipping, flipping, and we laughed because we couldn't speak each other's language, and the fish flung themselves about gasping for air they would not get, and we laughed—mine terrified, seeing but not fully comprehending that animals were indeed dying before my eyes—and finally the fish gave up and their eyeballs went milky and the boys and I were still laughing. Because, apparently, not speaking each other's language is funny.

Things died. I lived.

The Spanish boys' father owned a restaurant on the beach. That much I could translate. They would like to invite me to dinner, they said. One of the boys had a gold name bracelet with a ropy chain, the kind that were popular when I was in fourth grade, that said *Alex*. "Ah-LEESE," he said, and I said, *En inglés, Alicks*. I must, said Alex, eat with all his brothers and his father. I hoped they wouldn't mind that all I had left was my bikini. I had, apparently, discarded my silk bloomers before I climbed the mountain of eels. I imagined them, and my earring, washed out to sea, missing me, drowning.

That night I wore a bikini at a dinner table as if it was perfectly appropriate attire in which to meet a young man's family. I had no shame, and it continued to decrease the more of this ouzo thing they gave me. Alex poured some into a little glass of water. It made a brown swirl that looked like the corkscrew slide at White Water in Branson, the one that ripped up the butt of your swimsuit. *Bebelo,* said Alex. Drink. I did as I was told, repeatedly. They brought out the *paella* and I started to go for it, but first: *bebelo.* Next course, roasted chicken, *bebelo.* The Spaniards seemed mighty delighted to liquor up the redneck. But hey, when in . . . wherever I was. I drank.

When did the ouzo run out? How did the Swedes find me and drive me back to Barcelona? This I do not know, the memory irrevocably erased from my brain, but suddenly I was there, and Yael was brushing her hair before the mirror over the sink in which she peed. That night we sat in the same plaza where we sat the first night, eating ice cream, and I was babbling feverishly about something when I looked up and realized there was a giant pink Ferris wheel on a mountain in the distance. I lost my shit completely. Another mountain, another sign. What did this one want from me?

"Oh my god, an amusement park!" I shrieked. "Have you seen that?"

"Yeah," Yael says. "It's called Tibidabo."

I thought that she had said *Tippy-top-oh,* which of course it should be called since it was at the top of the mountain, and I was compelled to go to the Tippy-top-oh to ride the Ferris wheel. Its lights beckoned to me like beacon flamingos, like a gravity-defying trailer park.

"How do you get there?" I asked frantically. Yael spoke enough Spanish to ask somebody. He told us that something called the funicular (funicular! To transport one to the fun! Of course!) could usually take us, but since it was late at night we'd have to take a taxi to get there before it closed. Then there were some blotchy lights that may or may not have been real, and some loud music that also may or may not have been real, and I realized I was going very fast in a cab, and Yael for some reason was not there, and we went up up up. Maybe *this* was the mountain at the top of which I was supposed to have my epiphany. *It must be,* I thought. *This one has rides. It has a Ferris wheel on top, to get me even closer to the sky, where the aliens live, where I am supposed to be.*

We drove and drove at what seemed like a 90-degree angle. I closed my eyes and for a moment thought that when we got to the top we would be in Eureka Springs, a little hippie town in the Ozarks about an hour from Prairie Grove. Lately it had seemed entirely possible to me that when you closed your eyes, you might open them and find yourself somewhere else. Like, for example, on a spaceship. On another planet. Arkansas: another planet. I was not sure where I was or how I had gotten into the taxi. I focused on my breathing: *in, out, in, out,* if I counted every breath, I couldn't fly off somewhere else in my head. Or for real. Or whatever.

And then the car stopped and I stopped counting and opened my eyes. It was beautiful. I was on top of the city, I had made it to the very top of Barcelona all by myself, I did it, I did it,

I got away. There didn't seem to be anyone else there, which must have been because the park was either (a) a hallucination or (b) all for me. (When, years later, without knowing the story, a friend showed me a picture of her parents standing in front of the Tibidabo sign, I was stunned to learn that it was in fact a real place.) Either way. I breathed it in. I could smell the lights. I loved the way lights smelled. I felt very sorry for all the people who couldn't smell lights, who didn't have my magical powers. Later, I would learn that this was a Symptom, and would think, like so many medication-noncompliant mood-disordered people before me, *Well, it's kind of a fun one.*

But just as I started to walk toward the park, to dive into it, the lights started going out. One at a time, they vanished, like burst bubbles. I said "no," but then all the remaining lights went off at once and it was just me, alone, at the top of a dark mountain with no hands to hold me back.

They were turning it off, turning it off, I could smell it going out, it was like a million cigarettes extinguished at once, swallowing everything beautiful in leftover smoke.

"No," I said, "no, no, don't take it. Please don't take it." I was having trouble breathing because of the smell of the lights combined with the bass that was still stuck in my throat.

But it was gone. And I was alone. And I was way up high, with absolutely no idea how to get back down.

8

THE TATTOO PEOPLE *ask about the most is the Sanskrit that snakes around my neck. It's a yoga sutra,* Vitarka badhane pratipaksha bhavanam, *which means, When disturbed by disturbing thoughts, think of the opposite.*

I got it to remind me how lucky I am. I got it so that when I'm crying over some stupid breakup or lack of money or whatever passing bullshit is making me cry at the moment, I can look in the mirror and say to myself: Think of the opposite.

The trouble with mania of course, is, that depression always follows.

By the time I came home from London in August of 1989, I was so depressed I could hardly walk from the plane to the car. I was bloated and constipated from eating almost nothing but potatoes for the previous three weeks, a decision driven by a triumvirate of factors: one, they were the only alternative to the meat in the cafeteria, which was either gray or bloody depending on the day; two, I'd run out of money, so I couldn't afford to eat anywhere *but* the cafeteria; and three, it was what the aliens wanted me to do, having decided I'd had enough blueberry pie.

When my dad came to the Dallas airport to pick me up, I was all but catatonic. I had a backpack full of books, ticket stubs, and two mismatched shoes that had lost their mates somewhere along the way, and I was wearing the same tattered men's vest and white dress shirt I'd been wearing when I left. It was as if the trip had never happened. During my last week in London, knowing I was headed home, I assessed the situation and realized I hadn't changed as much as I'd wanted to. I wasn't going back to L.A. like Yael or an Ivy League university like Geoff or Africa like Lali. I was returning to Arkansas, where I had to pack up to go to college. I'd been accepted to Hendrix, the same place I'd gone to Governor's School a year before, and had gotten a full scholarship to cover my tuition. Even though it was four hours away from home, it was still in Arkansas. I'd applied and been accepted to Tulane, in New Orleans, where I wanted to go because it was Phil's alma mater. Though I'd spent my senior year applying for every scholarship I could find, the sum total of what I received was not enough that I could afford to attend school there. As I listened to my friends in London talk about Harvard and UCLA and Brown, I knew there was still a world of difference between us—they had money and came from a place where it was expected that one would go to a good school. When I told Yael I would be the first person on either side of my family to get a college education, she said, "No *way*," and proceeded to ask me if most people in Arkansas were illiterate. "Are you weird there because you wear shoes?" she asked. "If I moved there, would they burn a cross in my yard because I'm Jewish?"

We were gathered in someone else's dorm room at the time, a group of us American kids and our British friends, and everyone laughed. Yael said, "No, I'm serious, *would* they?" and everybody laughed more. Having British people laugh at me was mortifying, and thereafter I retreated to my bed— exhausted, broke, a hillbilly rube who didn't deserve to be there. I slept through my classes that last week. Upon returning home, the last thing I wanted to do was go live with yet another stranger in yet another dorm room. I wanted to live in a hole by myself. I was a groundhog, a gopher, a mole. I was so tired my bones hurt. All I wanted was peace and quiet and to sleep for eons.

I was sullen on the daylong road trip from Dallas back to Arkansas, dozing off and then snapping back to consciousness in an unexplainable panic. I could barely keep my eyes open, but I couldn't keep them shut either. It didn't seem worth sleeping, it didn't seem worth being awake. It didn't seem worth eating, communicating, or giving a shit. The thought of having to do those things ever again exhausted me to such a degree I felt like crying.

Back at my parents' house in Prairie Grove, I took a long bath, falling asleep and waking as I slipped underwater. I didn't feel like expending the energy required to pick up the soap, it seemed so pointless. I just wanted to lie in the hot water like a fetus, curled in my protective sac, with no responsibility to do anything except take in nourishment and kick once in a while. I stayed in until the water got cold and my skin wrinkled, sucked into itself as if I were vacuum-sealed inside. Then I got out of the tub and, without bothering to dry off, stared at my naked reflection in the mirror.

Ugly. That's what I was, fat and bloated and ugly and dull with a useless tongue as thick as a slab of butter. How was I supposed to go get a college education? I had nothing to say. I couldn't fit into any of my clothes. I couldn't learn anything. I didn't care. I had no questions, no ideas, no desire, no hunger. I thought about all the years of reading, of walking to and from class, of showering and eating surrounded by other people, of pretending like it meant something. I was supposed to go someplace and make something of myself, when I didn't even know if I had the energy to reach into the closet for a towel.

I went into my room and I lay on my bed, still naked and wet. I stared at the ceiling and I thought: *Today is the first day of the rest of my life.*

It made me cry.

I could swear the world was wrapped in a brown cloud the day I left for college. I felt like Pig-Pen in *Peanuts*, the kid whose vision is always obscured by his own filth. It was late August, with a high, bright sun, and kids were riding their bikes, and people were enjoying the last days of swimming pools and barbecues. I sunk into the backseat of my parents' packed Mercury, angry at my new comforter for being in a

plastic bag that kept sticking to my skin. I could smell the
mall coming through the bag, and I thought about the mall
and all the people in it, about the act of going somewhere and
picking something out and waiting in line to pay for it and
listening to other people's children scream and stomp because
they weren't getting whatever stupid plastic thing had last
entered their field of vision. My head pounded.

My roommate-to-be, Lindsay, had called me excitedly the
day after I came home from London, bubbling about matching
comforters and doing the entire room in black and white, and
what did I think about that? I said sure, whatever. Turns out
they had black-and-white bedding at JCPenney, and Lindsay
had already picked it out, and it cost blah blah blah, and the
sheets were blah blah blah, and beanbags and lamps blah blah.
My mom took me to Penney's and bought me the stuff Lindsay picked out, which made me feel guilty. I did not deserve
an education—after all, compared to my friends in England,
I was just some ignorant hill person going to an ignorant hill
school in an ignorant hill town, what could I possibly have to
offer the world? By the time we got to Hendrix, my parents
and I were barely speaking—at issue was something about me
being an ingrate—and I trudged up the stairs carrying boxes
of things I ostensibly needed. I wondered whether it was too
late to ask if I could live in a storage room and just sleep on a
stack of books.

I was indeed an ingrate, and Hendrix was and still is an
amazing school. But my depression obscured the truth. This is
why I feel frustrated now when I hear people referring to suicide as a self-centered act: of course it is. Nobody would com-

mit suicide if the pain of being inside herself, the agony of the sleepless, tortured hours spent watching the world get smaller and uglier, were bearable or could be relieved by other people telling her how they wanted her to feel. A depressed person is selfish because her self, the very core of who she is, will not leave her alone, and she can no more stop thinking about this self and how to escape it than a prisoner held captive by a sadistic serial killer can forget about the person who comes in to torture her every day. Her body is brutalized by her mind. It hurts to breathe, sleep, eat, walk, think. The gross maneuverings of her limbs are so overwhelming, so wearying, that the fine muscle movements or quickness of wit necessary to write, to actually *say* something, are completely out of the question.

I have spent almost every late summer of my adult life in exactly this depressed state. The summer of 1989 was the first time I experienced the hypomania of June and July followed by the devastating crash around Labor Day. Mood disorders tend to manifest themselves in this cyclical pattern. Many bipolar people report early-summer manias followed by predictable late-summer crashes. It is as if we plant our gardens in the spring, roll rapturously in our fields of brightly colored flowers a month later, and then discover, all too late, that we're severely allergic to what we've planted, and must retire to our beds to convalesce. We don't have to think about breathing through our noses when we're well, but the gasping for air consumes us when we're congested, and we can think of little else besides getting oxygen to our lungs. Forget dancing, scuba diving, running up a mountain, or any of the other things that differentiate living from existing; we're just struggling for basic respiration.

And so, I was selfish, because it was all I could be.

The one bright spot on the horizon that fall was that I somehow, inexplicably, arrived at Hendrix already having a boyfriend (male savior figure, exhibit 26, figure 4). Throughout my senior year of high school, I'd been writing long letters to Tommy, a friend from Governor's School, who wrote me long letters back. I'd fallen in love with him because we liked the same music, and because he was in love with me. Besides, he did slightly resemble Sting, with his little round glasses and spiky blond hair. I had driven across the state to his hometown of Jonesboro to accompany him to his senior prom; that night I had given him my first awkward, ill-informed blow job in a drive-through car wash, and afterward he told me he'd gotten into Hendrix too. He was going largely because I was, which should have been a warning sign. He had also applied to the University of New Orleans when he learned I was applying to Tulane, which should have been a blaring blue-light special of a warning sign. From Tommy I would learn the difference between a lover and a stalker, but at the time the latter simply seemed to me a more devoted version of the former.

So, my first day at Hendrix, as I made my twin-sized thin-mattressed bed with the mall-smelling comforter and prepared to crawl beneath it and never come out, Tommy came bounding into my room, all enthusiasm and horniness and a desire to get on with the exciting business of being a college student and being lovers. Lindsay had gone out for a fancy farewell dinner with her parents, so Tommy and I had sex on the black beanbag. I hadn't had sex in two years, since I found out Owen was cheating on me. Surprisingly, it hurt all over again, and I felt vaguely sick when it was over. My main memory of the experience is squinting against the setting sun glaring through the window, feeling like I'd somehow betrayed my body by revealing it before it was perfect. I was sweaty and sticky and uncomfortable and wanted to crank up the air conditioner, wash myself with very cold water, and shut my eyes against the world and all it entailed. Still, I told myself I loved Tommy, was *in love* with him, and tried valiantly to conjure the swooning feeling I'd had every time Owen touched me. I thought if I could feel something for someone, in the present moment, I'd know I was still alive, still human.

At least, I told myself, reaching gingerly between my legs, I was still able to feel physical pain. That was something. I have never been a cutter, but years later when I listened to the women in my DBT group talk about self-mutilation, I remembered that moment, and I understood.

Shortly thereafter, I stopped eating again. It really was that easy to fall back into the eating disorder. Terrifyingly easy, like falling back into the bed of a lover who's bad for you but turns you on like no one else. I quickly and easily lost the fifteen pounds I'd gained in England, and then some. I watched my weight fall to 110, 108, 105. I remembered the glory days of 98 and resolved to get to 96. One thing I learned that fall about depression: You could starve it away, at least temporarily. You could boil yourself down to a crystallized, self-contained, self-righteous entity, one to whom nothing mattered but how many calories were in the cereal.

I had a big brown cardigan sweater that became my ward-
robe that winter. I grew out my short hair, mostly because I
didn't have energy to get it cut. I also took birth control pills,
which made me cry over dog food commercials, thus manufacturing the only emotions I felt. At night I would snivel
over my books, wrapped in my sweater, my sheets, my comforter, Tommy. I would pull out of my closet the clothes my
mother had washed before I left home, the ones I hadn't worn
and Lindsay hadn't stolen, and attempt to breathe the Prairie
Grove out of them. I wrapped myself in my mother's smell:
Downy fabric softener and line-drying. The clothes were full
of our backyard, and they were my lifeline to a comfort I had
once felt. I was desperate for something to fill me up and reas-
sure me.

Compounding my guilt over my very existence were Tommy's unresolved feelings for Jesus. He had found the Baptist
church on his own, as a sad, searching kid with nonreligious
parents. Like me, he had gotten caught up in church-as-social-
life; unlike me, he embraced the prescribed guilt and refused
to shake it off. With increasing frequency, he cried after sex,
sitting at the foot of my bed with his face in his hands and berat-
ing himself for doing something Jesus told him not to. Hendrix
was a Methodist school with a Methodist chapel where services
were held on Sundays, but he found a local Evangelical church
and began attending regularly. I wonder now why I didn't put
my foot down about this, but assume it had something to do
with depression, anorexia, and a readiness—no, an eagerness,
unique to those with a penchant for self-destruction—to accept
that I was a bad person, a corrupter of others. I was far more

concerned with calories than human relationships, and I needed to feel guilty about something. Tommy gave me ample opportunity to beat myself up for having even the slightest libido, and motivation to starve it away.

By night, I wrote like my life depended on it, words my only passion other than thinness. I hunched beneath my lamp, contorting my body so the light warmed as much of me as possible. I was always so cold. Having all but given up on schoolwork, I poured myself into writing short stories, most of them about women with eating disorders. I painted pictures of the person I wanted to be, lengthy character sketches of girls who started out fat and ended up in the hospital, white sheets tight around their skeletons, feeding tubes stabbed into their throats. Their families stood around them saying, *Poor Celia, she died of an eating disorder.*

And then I found her: my muse. The girl whose polar opposite I could focus on becoming. Her name was Summer, and she was Tommy's ex-girlfriend. She was a year younger, still in high school in his hometown, Baptist, and a prude—although he'd broken up with her because he couldn't stand her mother, he held her up as the very picture of pious virginity. In fact, one evening in the cafeteria, he held up her picture for real: her mother, Jolene, had sent it to him.

"Her *mother* sent you her *senior picture?*" I asked with a vague dread that something very, very unpleasant was about to happen. What kind of mother sent pictures of her daughter to a boy who had dumped her for someone else (in this case, me?). Summer stared out at me from an Olan Mills portrait, chubby-cheeked, heavily made-up, bleached and permed to within an inch of her life. Her beady raisin eyes stared out of her doughy drop-biscuit face, framed by the ubiquitous fakebook backdrop of so many thousands of school photos. If there was one thing I hated, it was fake fucking books.

"Yeah," he said. "Jolene wants to make sure I don't forget her."

"Give me that picture," I said.

That night, I smeared glue stick all over the back of it and mounted it on a piece of orange construction paper. I emptied all the binge-and-purge food out of my fridge: the cookie dough, the Cap'n Crunch, the cellophane-wrapped slices of pasteurized processed American cheese food product. Into a garbage bag they went, along with the peanut butter Cap'n Crunch and the packets of ramen noodles purchased in bulk at Wal-Mart. Around Summer's picture I wrote with a fat black Sharpie: *Stacy's motivation to run five miles a day, every day, and stay under 2,000 calories a week!!* Then I stuck it to the empty fridge. Lindsay saw it and raised an eyebrow, but, having begun dating the campus drug dealer, she was too stoned to give me a lecture.

Tommy saw it, though. He said, "I don't think this is healthy."

"No duh," I said, and headed for the track. I was so far removed from kindness, compassion, reality, or sense that I motioned for Tommy to follow me—I'd equipped him with a disposable camera and asked him to take pictures of me from all different angles while I ran. He did, and I immediately took them to the one-hour photo and spent the evening studying them instead of whatever it was I should have been studying. That night, I hid the pictures under my mattress, to be pulled out the next time I needed a thrill: I had made pornography of myself, for myself. In the photos, the bones of my ribs showed in my back, which turned me on way more than Tommy ever could.

But we both needed someone to love us, however tepidly, so we stayed together. My family was so glad I had a boyfriend other than Owen, so glad I was in school, so glad I was finally normal and happy (because I couldn't tell them I was neither). I found a certain perverse comfort in being with someone whose self-loathing matched mine, even though his was driven by religion. Tommy's misery was a barometer against which to gauge my own—as long as I was more troubled than he was, I was winning.

One evening, Lindsay introduced me to grain alcohol mixed with diet orange soda, with a side order of bong hits. I hadn't had any alcohol since England, and once I started drinking and getting high, it felt so nice to be out of my head. Plus, it made Lindsay think I was cool. She couldn't stand Tommy, and asked me frequently why I was with "that religious fanatic dork." Their loathing for each other was mutual; Tommy saw her as a heinous sinner. Feeling that I needed to "loosen up and tie one on," Lindsay invited me to go with her to a party that night. Recklessly, I said yes. I'd been skipping parties all year, partly because alcohol had calories and partly because I didn't want to hear it from Tommy. But, to use Lindsay's phraseology, I decided to "just say *fuck it*, dude." When Tommy called to see if I wanted to go to Steak 'n' Shake, I told him I already had plans.

"With Lindsay?" he asked.

"Yes," I said.

"Lindsay is an alcoholic whore," he said, and hung up. I stared at the receiver, feeling simultaneously exhilarated and guilty. After all, it wasn't like anyone else loved me; I should take what I could get. I should be grateful. In an effort not to think about it, I ate some leftover pizza Lindsay had left in the fridge. I'd been trying to ignore it all day. There was half of it left. I devoured it in under ten minutes. I purged, put on a black dress, and met Lindsay in her boyfriend Neil's dorm room, where he sat surrounded by a cloud of sandalwood incense, weighing out dime bags beneath a Led Zeppelin poster.

The party was at Neil's friend's place in an apartment complex just off campus, and it was already going full tilt when we got there. Most of the guests were either comatose on the couch or making out with one another. I chased the lingering taste of vomit with a shot glass of vodka, then another, then another. By the time Tommy came to find me, I was wasted in the apartment complex parking lot, yelling at Lindsay through the chain-link fence over which she had leapt after taking too much acid. She and Neil had dropped before I arrived, and were now under the impression they were being chased by wild dogs. On the other side of the fence, they screamed, giggled, slapped each other, and used the word "dude" to express a range of emotions.

I knew I was in trouble. I stood up, teetered, looked around for help. Two guys in a yellow station wagon blared "Ice, Ice

Baby" on the stereo so their friend could break-dance on the hood.

"Hey," I said, trying to act sober.

Tommy looked at me with such intense disgust I felt my stomach churn in shame. Or maybe it was the fact that I'd barfed up all my food and drunk several different kinds of alcohol in rapid succession, that could have been it too. All I knew was that this wasn't me. I should be home writing, studying, making the most of my education, excelling. But now I was just like every other stupid drunk college student on the planet.

I don't remember what we said, I just remember that I shoved him, and he shoved me back, and I fell into the fence. I was so ashamed of myself, so appalled by my behavior. That night, I did strenuous drunken calisthenics in my room, as if enough leg lifts and crunches could absolve me. I did not eat. Instead, I knelt before the fridge as if it were an altar, stared at Summer's picture, and resolved to be better. Her fat cheeks and slight double chin did nothing to convince me that I was thinner, and the more I dwelt on her fatness, the more I felt my own body grow in response. I couldn't possibly be thinner than anybody. If Summer was fat, I was fatter. Even as I cupped my hands around my hip bones, lay on my back and felt my ribs, saw my abdomen sinking toward my spine, I knew Summer was skinnier. You could have stood her right beside me on a scale and wrapped measuring tapes around us both, and I would have told you there was something wrong with the scales and the measuring tapes. Later I would find out that this sort of dissociation is common to borderlines, and that in fact there is a name for it: "splitting." For some reason, we have a uniquely difficult time seeing the world as anything other than black or white, "all good" or "all bad." Incorporating both positive and negative beliefs about a person, including oneself, is largely impossible. We see ourselves and others in an all-or-nothing way: I was not just fat, but *the fattest*. Nobody else on the planet could possibly be fatter, and if units of measure said otherwise, the units of measure were wrong. Of all the things that go on in my head, this has always been the hardest to explain to so-called normal people, and by far the most painful aspect of the illness. Nobody wants to hate herself all the time, it's just that some of us, unfortunately, feel compelled to. When you operate from an assumption that everyone is better than you, you tend to punish yourself for not measuring up. Because Summer was a Baptist virgin cheerleader and I was a godless heathen sex-haver who had been rebuked by a curling iron the one time I dared to hold a pom-pom, she was better, which meant she was thinner.

Flawless logic, right?

The following Monday morning, when Tommy knocked on my door to walk me to class, I saw that he had with him a copy of the Alcoholics Anonymous handbook. "It's from Jolene," he said. "She overnighted it."

Jolene wanted Tommy to marry Summer as soon as she got out of high school. It still happened regularly in Arkansas that a girl was married by eighteen and a mother by twenty, and if arranged marriages were legal, Jolene would have hunted him down, locked him in the back of a windowless van with a rented tuxedo, and hauled him straight to the Baptist church.

"To you?"

"To *you*. In care of me."

"Your ex-girlfriend's mother sent you a copy of the Alcoholics Anonymous handbook to give to *me*?"

He nodded. Flabbergasted, I took the book. My indignation was overtaken by mortification. Tommy had told Jolene I was a sinner, and she had seen fit to issue forth in short order an attempt to save my soul.

Because I couldn't force myself to believe in God, I sublimated my guilt by jogging as many miles a day as I could—at least five—as penance, until my muscles quivered so hard I couldn't continue. By the end of my run, I would be scooting along on my toes, going something like a quarter of a mile an hour. It was all about endurance. The one thing I knew for sure was that if I was running, I wasn't doing anything wrong; I wasn't, in that moment, failing myself or anyone else. As much as my muscles and my heart ached, exercise was a welcome respite. My drive to succeed, and my conviction that I never would, led to more and more nights sitting awake slugging coffee and chain-smoking. In utter despair, I wrote stories I subsequently thought were shit and tore up, trying to prove myself to myself and knowing I never could. The more I jacked myself up on caffeine and nicotine, the more I exercised, the more weight I lost, the more irrelevant sleep became. I simply didn't need it anymore, just like I didn't need food. All those people who said you needed both to survive were wrong—I could live on sheer determination, pure force of will, adrenaline, and air. My wheels spun faster and faster, and the mania, of course, came back. It was subtle at first—the wind in the trees became a little louder, the rustling leaves scratched insistently at my eardrums, and the carrots on the salad bar turned a little more orange. My professors began to sound like Charlie Brown's teacher, their voices garbled; what they wanted from me was indecipherable. When it came time to register for spring classes, I decided on a whim to take two senior-level English courses and French. I had never taken French in my life, but I felt confident I could go right into French II, because I was pretty sure I had the magical power to divine foreign languages.

My mother called me one day to tell me that the high school yearbooks from my senior year had come in, that she had received mine and would mail it soon. They were always published in the fall semester, a document of the previous rather than current school year, and I was excited to see it, as I had been the editor. When Tommy came over that night, I told him my yearbook was on the way. "I hope it looks okay," I said.

He was quiet for a minute, and then he said, "It does. You did a good job."

I paused for a moment to make sure I'd heard him right. "How do you know?"

"I have one," he said.

"You ordered my yearbook?"

"No," he said, and hung his head. "Jolene did."

With that, he pulled it out of his backpack, as I tried to comprehend what had happened: Jolene had looked up the number for my school. She had called and asked to speak to the journalism teacher. She had paid money to get my high school yearbook and study my photos. I snatched the book from him and opened it. Inside the front cover, Jolene had written:

Tommy,
She's a very pretty girl. We're sure you'll be happy.
With love,
Jolene and Summer

Tucked inside was Summer's most recent cheerleading picture, in which she had clearly lost weight.

The world broke apart again, another shattering. All the instruments in the song on the radio separated, and I dropped the book and shook and sweated. Then I bolted, leaving him standing there, and I ran out through the lobby of the dorm and kept going until I reached the track. I was barefoot.

There's nothing quite like being manic and sliding into obsession and then realizing the people you're obsessed with are obsessed with you too. It's a strange inverse psychosis, like seeing your reflection thrown back at you in a thousand mirrors, going on forever, and it wreaks havoc on successful splitting, which may be a really fucked-up defense mechanism, but is nevertheless your one method of making sense of the world. I ran around the track that night until my bare feet burned and I fell, exhausted, heart pounding so hard it threatened to explode, into the cool wet grass. Lay there for a while, pulled myself up, walked gingerly back to the dorm, went to the bathroom to pee out all the gallons of water I was in the habit of drinking. Coming out of the stall, I saw my reflection in the mirror, and pressed my nose up against my own face. I stood like that for a long time, knowing that if I just remained in contact with the girl in the mirror, if we just kept our noses pressed together, I wouldn't lose her. Maybe that girl staring back at me, the one with the bright green irises glowing in the bloodshot eyes, the one with coffee-stained teeth and cigarette-stained fingers, whose hair hung in her face, whose collarbones protruded, maybe she was disappointed in me too. I knew we were supposed to have something to do with each other, but as I stood there staring at her, I couldn't remember what it was. I was completely dissociated; I felt nothing. My fingers couldn't feel my cheeks, my cheeks couldn't feel my fingers. Someone had cut the wires. I was nothing but an apparition.

I dug my fingernails into my face. The girl in the mirror did too, and she left red marks. I kept clawing. Our skin, our faces, our bodies were all make-believe—we had no shell. We were permeable membranes. We had been scraped raw by our own hands. Anything could get in and infect us.

From that day forward, I was on the run. Nothing and nobody moved fast enough. If I didn't keep moving, I'd break down. I went to class, but nothing made sense. In French I stared at the words with their twelve million silent vowels and for some reason the ones that ended in *eaux* made me laugh. I would sit there learning nothing and trying not to crack up at how the French spelled Ø.

One day my teacher called on me and I had to speak in front of everyone. I tried, but I couldn't make any words. So I said something in Spanish: *cabeza de aire*, airhead. My Spanish teacher in high school had called me that once when he caught me writing a story instead of conjugating verbs.

Everyone started laughing except me. I started crying. Wailing. Like someone had just died. My professor looked alarmed. I ran from the room and never went back.

When I went to drop the class, it was too late. Not only did I have to remain in the class, my advisor informed me that I currently had a 3.4 GPA, needed a 3.5 to keep my scholarship for the following year, and that if I got anything less than a B in French I'd lose it.

How could anyone be so worthless? shrieked my brain, which, interestingly, had taken on Jolene's screeching Southern accent, the one I'd heard on Tommy's answering machine. *How could anyone, so much, so very, very much, deserve to die?* Because it was all I knew to do, I went to my room, hid in the closet—making sure to sit on a pile of shoes—and covered my body with words in Sharpie marker: everything mean everybody had ever said to me. For good measure, I wrote the word *FAT* in every empty space.

Not surprisingly, I failed French, and I did indeed lose my scholarship. But I also lost weight, so none of those things mattered as much as they should have. On the last day of school, having had exactly enough of Jolene and the fundamentalist thing, I broke up with Tommy. I told him I wasn't coming back, packed my stuff in my Mustang, called Phil Thornton in Fayetteville, scheduled an appointment for the following day, and drove off into the proverbial sunset, saying goodbye to another dream sacrificed to madness.

Interstate 40 goes on forever. You can drive it almost straight from Conway to Prairie Grove, where your parents, who are by this point justifiably afraid of you and your moods, may or may not be waiting. You can drive until there's nothing on the radio but the Christian stations, and keep going until there's nothing but static. Until even Jesus finally gets bored and bails.

Back in Prairie Grove, hopeless and depressed, I slept in a scrawny, weeping ball on my parents' couch for two weeks. When I dragged myself to my appointment with Phil, he informed me gently but firmly that curling up and dying was not an option. He made me call him daily and report to him what I'd eaten, focusing more on the eating disorder than the attendant depression. He also talked me into getting a job— which I forced myself to do in order to please him—at a punk clothing store in Fayetteville. I liked the store and the people, and quickly developed a crush on a boy I met there, which, like so many loves before and since, instantly elevated my mood. Borderlines have a tendency to fall epically in and out of love on a regular basis, and to experience wild mood swings based upon the actions of the beloved. Lile Copeland wore a fedora, played the trumpet, and took black-and-white pictures with old, strange cameras, and as a result, the world that had been black the week before was suddenly shiny and new, and I the happiest girl alive.

In an expansive in-love display of impulsivity, when I went to enroll at the University of Arkansas in Fayetteville, I registered as a theater major. I'd been watching films starring Helen Mirren and thinking a lot about the plays I'd seen in London, and Lile had recently revealed a crush on Carole Lombard, so I figured I might as well pursue my sudden, intense passion for acting. (This was the second manic episode; one good indicator of oncoming mania, learned from going through it enough damn times: the number of sudden, intense new passions I feel I must immediately pursue.) But the desire to become an actress had more urgent and sinister underpinnings—after all, if you don't have a self, you can at least stand onstage and pretend to be somebody else. It seemed the best option, the only option. I poured myself into acting, I poured acting into myself, I assured my parents I was fine, and of course I neglected to call Phil Thornton. I didn't need therapy, after all. Who needs a shrink when she's not depressed?

9

XENON TALKED, WHICH *made it the most terrifying and fasci-*
nating pinball game in the Land of Oz arcade in the Northwest
Arkansas Mall. The back glass featured a blue woman's face
with huge red-and-yellow eyes, and when you walked up to the
machine she said, "Welcome to Xenon." The first time I saw it, at
age eight, I ran screaming.

Years later, still haunted by the memory, I researched the
game and found that the voice of Xenon was actually electronic
musician Suzanne Ciani. In 1979, using computer chips the size
of dominos, motherboards the size of floor tiles, and synthesizers
with tangles of patch cables like ropes of red licorice, she sat at
her monochromatic Texas Instruments computer and created a
voice for a machine.

Of course once I knew this, being the mad science junkie I am, I had to have a Xenon tattoo. Her otherworldly blue face became part of the sleeve of female robots inked onto my left arm by Emma Porcupine. Inspired by a book I brought her about the now-defunct Museum of Questionable Medical Devices, she gave Xenon a phrenology helmet.

It fits her. And once again, something that scared me is exorcised, incorporated, with me forever.

Fall 1990 was a brief respite between mania and depression, the kind that get shorter and shorter the longer you leave bipolar disorder unattended, during which I found myself wearing a nun's habit, singing "Ave Maria" in the dark. I felt like I would lose my breath, pee myself, pass out cold. I grabbed the black velvet curtain to steady myself and it gave off a great poof of dust. My face smelled like expired Ben Nye makeup, and the blood bag tucked beneath my armpit was sticky from sweat. Behind me Trudy Bennett cleared her throat, as if to remind me one last time that she was supposed to play Agnes of God for her thesis role and everyone knew I'd unfairly usurped it.

"Mother Miriam," I said, and stepped onto the stage, raw and naked and brightly lit. I was an *actress*! My mission in life was to make everyone in the theater believe me, to make Burke White, the director, love me, and to keep the trick stigmata from going off before its time. And, of course, to show Trudy Bennett that I could by god do this, even though she was a grad student and I only a sophomore. I'd heard all the things she'd said about how terrible I was in the role—were theater majors ever not gossiping, or running off to report that gossip to the person it was about?——and I was deeply hurt and determined to prove her wrong.

But that night, at that moment, everything was sublime. I knew, for the first time in my life, exactly where I was and what I was supposed to be doing. I had a script. I had a costume. I was Agnes of God.

When I first met Burke White, I was dumping blue powdered Fresh Start laundry detergent into an industrial washing machine at Hogwash, the Laundromat just down the hill from the University of Arkansas. By the time I put my clothes in the dryer, his eyes were burning a hole in my back. I felt his gaze travel from my hair down my spine to my ass, and it was strangely warm and pleasant, like an oversized bath towel or a blow dryer or a hug. I shivered. I turned around.

"Hi," I said, and he nodded.

He wore glasses and loafers and a sweater worthy of Bill Cosby, and his salt-and-pepper hair just brushed his eyebrows. He was distinguished in a professorly way, and I fell into a dirty-old-man-father-figure fantasy that left me tingling as I gathered my laundry and walked home.

The next time I saw him was at my first audition as a new theater student at the U of A. Again, it made me tingle when he looked at me. I tried out for the role of Thea in *Hedda Gabler*, doing a woefully mischosen monologue from *Who's Afraid of Virginia Woolf?* I stumbled around the black box, a fake-drunk nineteen-year-old Martha in a fluffy pink sweater.

When I finished my faux-drunken tirade, the room was largely silent. The professor directing *Hedda Gabler* blinked hard several times before saying "Thank you" in a tone that suggested what she actually meant was, *Please leave the theater. Not the building, the profession.* Mortified, I turned to run for the nearest bathroom, lock myself in a stall, and sob in abject humiliation. But the man from Hogwash was standing in the doorway. He had seen the entire thing. He had witnessed my flailing, my utter lack of sophistication.

"Do you sing?" he asked.

I wasn't quite sure how to answer. Did he mean, *Do you sing as badly as you act?* Or did he mean that he had seen something in me, some hidden magic, that I didn't see in myself, and if I sang that would make it complete? Better yet, perhaps he meant, *Will you sing show tunes while doing the dance of the seven veils at the foot of my bed after we make sweet love?*

"Sure," I said.

"Sing something," said Burke. My mouth opened and I stared into his eyes and belted out "I Want to Marry a Lighthouse Keeper" from the *Clockwork Orange* soundtrack.

He stared at me.

"Hmmm," he said.

The next morning, as if there was any hope, I slunk into the greenroom to read the cast lists. *Hedda Gabler* was, as expected, going on without me. The list for *Agnes of God* consisted only of the names of the actresses playing Mother Miriam and Dr. Livingstone. Trudy and her friends, including the icy Annie, who had been cast as Hedda, stood whispering among themselves.

"You'll get it," said Annie, laying her hand on Trudy's shoulder. Trudy nodded and slammed a Diet Coke.

As I stood fantasizing about Burke fucking Agnes backstage with her habit over her head, my new friend Rob, a
250-pound bald drag queen who went by the name Sofonda
Peters, walked up and invited me to lunch. We headed off for
some chicken fingers with ranch dressing in the cafeteria, but
as we passed Burke's office, I once again saw him standing in
the doorway, studying me. He caught my eye and nodded me
inside. Everything stopped: my breath, my central nervous
system, time.

He didn't speak, or if he did, I didn't hear him. The room
smelled like Marlboros and textbooks baked in the sun.
The metal wheels of his big leather chair sang the short roll
toward his desk, and as he pulled open a wooden drawer, I half
expected it to shoot forth a beam of glowing light and melt our
faces like in *Raiders of the Lost Ark*. He took out a script and
slid it across the desk to me. He didn't look up.

"First rehearsal's Monday"—he lit a cigarette—"Agnes."
He gave me the smallest of grins.

I stood there mute until Sofonda smacked me.

There was a suspended sparkling hour that day when
Sofonda and I sat at lunch together, when we were the only
ones who knew, before Trudy found out. Everything about that
day is frozen, still: the dead-leaf smell mingled with the cafeteria grease every time someone opened the door, the little
brown crumbs, the chicken fingers left in the cups of thick
white dressing, the too-loud cackling laugh of my large and
sweaty companion, who mopped his blushing bald head with
his napkin. I remember the smears on the dirty table, the way
I folded up a piece of notebook paper to stick beneath its unsta-

ble leg. The pristine blue Dramatists script before me, *Agnes of God* in italics on its cover. The thrill of borrowing a high-lighter and sweeping across my lines with fluorescent yellow. But most of all I remember how Burke looked when he first believed in me.

I kept that script beside my bed for a long time, long after rehearsals had ended and the play had closed, because I wrote every word Burke said on the grubby pages like gospel. I felt as though, having been granted the honor of his direction, I had joined a secret society that had formerly granted member-ship only to girls like Trudy and Annie. Burke had trademark sayings those who had been directed by him tossed back and forth among themselves, a shorthand the cool kids spoke, and now I knew their passwords. For example, if someone wasn't performing up to par, wasn't really "in character," you could tell him or her to "try forestry," because if you weren't going to devote yourself completely to being an actor you might as well give up now and do something else. Or if a scene wasn't going well, you would tell the actors to "bag it," which was Burkespeak for "cut." If your actors seemed lazy, you would yell, "BIGGER LOUDER FASTER!" But the best thing about Burke, the thing we all wanted to emulate most of all, was how dramatic and sexy he made chain-smoking and constant swearing.

We all worshiped him, everyone in the department, and we competed for his attention like Girl Scouts selling cook-ies to earn our way to camp. We all wanted to be able to say "Fuck!" in as many hilarious intonations as he did; we wanted to blow smoke out our nostrils for punctuation. During the

day, I shared Burke with other people, but alone at night, I
closed my eyes and conjured his face and kept him for myself.
His words put their hands all over me.

I had exactly two female friends at the U of A. Dana, a dramatically pale, dramatically thin grad student with ice-blue
eyes that bulged out of her head and skin so translucent you
could almost see her bones, glanced at me across the greenroom one day, smiled, and walked up and introduced herself.
She designed the lighting for all Burke's shows, and she quickly
became my older, wiser ally in the department. She was calm
and unfazed, and no matter how much I freaked out, her presence always calmed me down. She liked me in spite of the fact
that I was so frequently manic and terrified of whether or not
other people found me smart or talented or beautiful or whatever. She had an actual Buddhist shrine in her apartment. I
marveled at her ability to meditate, and occasionally wished
that I, like she, had lupus, and could achieve her degree of otherworldly skinniness.

My other friend, Polly, was Dana's total opposite, a wiry
aspiring playwright who stayed up late into the night doing
shots of Jack Daniel's, chain-smoking the generic cigarettes
that already smelled like stale butts while they were still
burning, and tapping out endless revisions of her masterwork
about the last hours of River Phoenix.

Shortly after I met Polly, we became roommates, moving
into a ramshackle rental house. Our dark brown carpet was
matted from the feet of too many tenants, the whole place
smelled like smoke and mildew, and the curtains were made of
black fabric printed with Jim Beam bottles, except in the living

room where the drafty window was blocked by a pilled beige blanket with a picture of a bear eating a fish. It was $200 a month, and it was an entire house all to ourselves, which made it luxurious in our eyes.

"I think the parallels between River and the Virgin Mary are striking," Polly would holler boozily from her room when I woke up to pee. She'd lure me in for "just one cigarette, come on," and then expound at length about how the set was going to look like the *Pietà*.

One night, shortly after I was cast as Agnes, Dana came over for whiskey and beers and a game of Risk. As we downed our second six-pack, she revealed the riveting information that Burke was her M.F.A. thesis chair and she went to his house for their meetings.

"You've been in his *house*?" I whispered, incredulous.

"Oh sure," she said.

"What does it *look* like?"

"Well, there are pictures of his dead wife everywhere."

"Dead WIFE?" I gasped. My god, Burke became a more tragic and romantic figure by the minute.

"Yeah, she died of cancer five years ago."

"What was her name?"

"Jillian."

Jillian White. Jillian Mrs. Burke White. Mrs. Wife of Burke.

The job opening for the position of Burke's wife inspired the bulk of my sexual fantasies throughout the rehearsal of *Agnes*. I ate, slept, and breathed my lines. I attended two Catholic church services in hopes of more authentic characterization, coming away with little more than bruised kneecaps and the smell of incense in my coat. I sang hymns naked in front of my mirror, running my hands over my body. At rehearsals, when Burke gave us notes, I gazed at him with an expression I hoped conveyed the dual sentiments of *I'm listening very carefully to everything you say,* and *Take me, I'm yours.*

I sat on Polly's bed in the middle of the night with a joint in one hand and a cigarette in the other and detailed for her my obsessive repertoire of Burke and Jillian White fairy tales. She half listened while scribbling notes about the striking similarities among River Phoenix, Dracula, and Gandhi, occasionally reminding me to pass the joint. Eventually the conversation would degenerate into silence and we'd end up sitting in front of the TV watching late-night movies and eating Cool Whip out of the tub, and these were the fantasies that got us through the night.

Being an actress was intoxicating and sensual, and I confused it with sex, which seemed the only experience comparable in intensity. Being onstage, like being in bed, consumed all my attention and provided an outlet for the boundless manic energy that had, by that point, seated me shotgun in the race car of my psyche. Putting on my costume was a divine ritual; when I looked in the mirror and saw myself as a nun, I could almost believe I was holy. Burke was God, and I was his supplicant marionette.

For once, people approved of what I did. Every night, for six divine nights, I walked out for the curtain call covered in corn-syrup blood for the world to see, and sometimes my audience stood up and clapped until I bowed again, and again, and again. Polly and Dana carried roses to the foot of the stage and offered them up to me, and I leaned over the footlights to take them. I pulled off a rosebud and broke the barrier between my fake church and the secular house, tossing petals over the threshold to rain down on my laughing friends' heads. After the show Burke hugged me, and he leaned into my ear and, in a reference to the habit I wore, whispered in his low sweet voice, "Nice work, little penguin." I lived for those hugs, every night until the show closed, six treasured embraces, six times folded into his healing blanket arms.

On a Sunday, after the final matinee, our stage crew began to tear down the set. I watched the walls that had held me safe dismantled before my eyes. Burke, my deity, walked out into the parking lot, got into his brown Nissan, and, just that easily, my latest God was gone. I walked home alone, carrying the wilting flowers that had adorned my dressing room table. They seemed sad, so I didn't want to throw them away. I thought I'd dry them and hang them over my bed like an upside-down shrine.

At home, I left the vases on my bedroom floor while I ran a bath. It wasn't until I saw the sticky fake blood redden the water that I realized I couldn't get clean enough. I wanted anything that would remind me of the show off of me. I wanted to wash away Burke's last hug and admit to myself that he was at home right now without me, that I wasn't really going to be his lover. I felt stupid for having had such a crush on him. He hadn't taken me home that night to hold next to him in bed, hadn't even hugged me any longer than he'd hugged Mother Miriam or Dr. Livingstone, hadn't said any special goodbyes.

I turned on the shower, clutched my knees to my chest, and cried as the bathtub filled. I could scald my skin, pelt myself with hot-needle rain, abrade my flesh with all the loofahs in the world, it didn't matter, I wasn't Agnes anymore.

I turned the shower off. I opened the drain. My fake blood whirlpooled away like spilled jewels. I left soggy footprints on the bedroom carpet because drying off seemed like a ridiculous waste of time.

I made a ring of flowers around me and fell asleep hugging my script. When I woke up, some of its blue cover had rubbed off on my breasts, there was turquoise morning light, my teeth were chattering, and the blooms all around me had turned to brown. But I still hadn't let go.

Burke never cast me again. There was always some new girl; he picked us like hopeful daisies. When it was Polly's turn—when she was cast in a Neil Simon play, offered a role to which Dana had insisted on referring, for weeks beforehand, as "the Stacy Pershall role"—I seethed for days. I *knew* I was better. After all, Polly's voice cracked and squeaked from her constant smoking, she couldn't enunciate, and she wasn't an actress anyway, she was a *playwright*. But what really killed me was what Burke said to me just after the audition.

I was bouncing around in the hallway, trying to burn off some excess energy so I could be focused in case he asked me to read again, when I felt his presence behind me. I smelled him first, Old Spice and Marlboros. I tried to turn around coolly, not to let him see that when he stood so close it made me shake.

"Stacy," he said, "who would *you* cast?"

ME, my brain screamed, *me me me, because I love you and I need another chance to make you fall in love with me.* But I knew he was telling me he'd decided on someone else. "Polly?" I choked.

He nodded. "You and I have had our bond. With *Agnes.*"

He walked away to write the cast list.

For the next six weeks, as they rehearsed, I swallowed furious tears when I saw him call Polly into his office. I ached to know what went on behind that door. One day, I saw her follow him inside, and because there happened not to be anyone else around at the moment, I crept up to the door and pressed my ear against it.

Behind a closed door, a man old enough to know better proved that he did not. And on the other side, I learned one of life's most important lessons: When you find your gods are fallible, the best thing to do is forget.

10

ON MY LEFT *calf I have a tattoo of an old-timey telephone made of bones. Around it, in elaborate four-color curlicue script, it says,* Wait! Don't answer it!

This one came about when Denise became obsessed with the "missed connections" section of Craigslist. One night she called me and said, "Listen to this one. This girl moved into an apartment where an old man died. Now when she comes home at night, her underwear is scattered all over her bedroom, and she thinks his ghost is responsible. So her ad says, 'Me: girl who pays $1,500 a month to live here. You: guy who answered the bone phone and needs to move on.'" Denise, being easily entertained, is always up for a new euphemism for death.

For the next several months, whenever she calls me and I don't

answer, she leaves messages in a voice I think is her attempt at an
impression of Vincent Price: "Fiend! It's a good thing you didn't
answer, because this is the bone phone! If you had answered it,
you would have turned into bones and died! Or died and turned
into bones! Whichever!"

I was sick, and getting sicker. By the spring of 1993, the end
of my senior year, I was existing on peanut butter Cap'n Crunch
and blue Kool-Aid, exercising several hours a day, barely sleeping, and still living with Polly in our wood-paneled house saturated with the smell of cigarette smoke and, on rainy days, the
previous tenant's dog. I was completely nuts, and had long since
stopped getting cast in plays—as Burke said, I was "too vola-
tile." I had stopped seeing Phil sometime in my sophomore year,
because I knew I was going *really truly crazy,* and since he had
described me (actress me, when I ran into him once in an up
period) as one of his "success stories," I knew I couldn't bear to
let him down. I stopped seeing the one person who was perhaps
best equipped to help me, because I didn't want him to know I
needed help.

The theater department consisted, at that point, of a few
people who somehow, inexplicably, liked me, and a lot who,
with good reason, thought I was a narcissistic anorexic brat. In
truth, I was needy, desperate, and hyperactive, utterly terrified
of slowing down and facing the emptiness inside me. Those
who counted themselves among my few friends (bless them)
became my emergency support system by default. They, like
my parents, were exhausted by my constant flitting into and
out of therapy (with a string of frightened psychology grad

students at the university counseling center, who largely just
sat there while I rattled off my Brilliant Plans at breakneck
speed or wailed inconsolably about my latest breakup), my
total refusal of all psychiatric medications after a bad experience with lithium, and the constant drama that surrounded
me everywhere I went.

One night, our secrets about Burke still unspoken, Polly sat
at the kitchen table smoking and reading a magazine. I had
developed a habit of tensing one calf muscle over and over
again, or both calf muscles like *right left right left right,* or tapping the floor with one pinkie toe and then the other. I imagined that my taps were drawing figure eights on the floor, then
I imagined the figure eights catching fire.

Polly kept looking at me.

"What?"

"Stop shaking the table."

I huffed, got up, poured myself some blue Kool-Aid, sat back
down, tried not to tap. She looked up at me again.

"What?"

"Nothing."

"*What?*"

"I'm reading something that makes me think of you." She
paused, studying my face as if trying to determine just how
far over the edge telling me what she thought might push me.
"Have you ever heard of borderline personality disorder?"

As a matter of fact, I had, and when she said it I felt something in me plummet. I read psychology books all the time in
the campus bookstore, instead of going to Western Civ, and
tried to figure out what was wrong with me. I had practically

memorized the entirety of the Axis I and Axis II diagnoses in the DSM. I knew about borderline personality disorder, and I know it couldn't be cured. I knew that psychiatrists often refused to treat borderline patients because they were hopeless.

"Nope, never heard of it," I said. "What is it?"

She read me the diagnostic criteria. "I'm just saying," she said, trying with all her might to put it gently, obviously afraid of my reaction, "that it sounds a lot like you."

"Hmm," I said, and continued tapping. "I don't really think so."

"Okay," she said, though I knew she thought it was not okay at all.

In the spring of 1993 everyone was watching me fall apart. Part of me, shamefully, liked it. It seemed such a natural thing to do, finally attempting suicide. The time had come, and I knew it. All I needed was a definite preceding event, a point in the drama in particular need of punctuation.

Given that my life was, by that point, constant, high-pitched drama, I didn't have to wait long for the big moment. Having filled the void where a self should have been with one acting role after another, I auditioned with a desperation that led to my not getting cast at all. I was seen as the talented but deal-breakingly unstable girl, and none of my professors or fellow students wanted to work with me. My careening moods, which caused very real pain and anguish—often evidenced by frequent and inappropriate crying fits in class, over such travesties as not being able to learn lines for an assigned scene—were seen as cries for attention, something over which I had control.

I had a job waiting tables but was abysmal at it, too overstimulated, frantic, and distractible to keep up with refilling water and turning orders in to the kitchen.

The one thing I was living for, my last semester in college, was my move to Ohio that summer. I had auditioned at a regional festival in the fall and been selected as one of ten acting interns for the '93–'94 season at the Ensemble Theatre of Cincinnati, which I viewed as The Big City. I wanted to believe that as soon as I got out of Arkansas everything would be fine, that my mental illness was due solely to being misunderstood by rednecks, which they certainly would not have just across the river from Kentucky. I struggled in vain to keep it together enough to finish my last few classes and function well enough at my job to save money for my move.

The downfall: I couldn't control my temper. Having inherited my father's white-hot rage, I did two things within a week's time that gave me ample reason to attempt suicide: I yelled at my boss, in the middle of a full dining room, that he was a jackass, and was justifiably fired, and I tried to run over a group of student parking attendants for giving me a ticket I didn't feel I deserved. One of the things I've read about borderlines is that we alternate between a sense of entitlement and the belief that we're lower than the dirt under people's shoes. I felt I should be allowed to park in a no-parking zone because it was in the theater lot, and I was a theater major. Angry that these freshmen with ticket pads didn't see my logic, I swerved at them as I drove out of the lot. Brought before the university disciplinary committee the following day, I argued that I didn't really intend to hit them, I was just going to teach them a lesson. They told me they would have to discuss whether or not to expel me, and let me know that, had I not been two credits away from graduation with plans to move out of the state, they would not have needed to discuss it at all. When, the following day, I was fired from my job—my boss did not hesitate to use the word "crazy" when telling me why I was being dismissed—I went home and started taking pills.

I burst through the door and realized Polly wasn't home, as evidenced by the fact that there was no smoke billowing from her room, and had a brief moment of hesitation over the fact that there was no one there to rescue me. It meant, however, that I could eat all her pills, all the antidepressant samples stashed in her kitchen cabinet (Polly, who also had a history of depression had a habit of seeing shrinks—M.D.'s who could prescribe drugs, not clinical psychologists like Phil—getting drugs, and discontinuing them at the first sign of side effects). Even though the thought of medication terrified me, I grabbed a box of Pamelor, popped out the capsules, and chewed them, tasting the bitter sandy grit as they turned to gelatinous goo in my mouth. I figured they'd hit my bloodstream faster that way; none of that time-release shit. I ate every pill in the cabinet, and as I stared at the pile of boxes and foil packs scattered at my feet, my vision began to blur. Dizzy, I stumbled toward the kitchen table, thinking that if I just crawled under it, if I just curled up in a ball, I would have a heart attack and die in peace, a compact little package Polly could tie up neatly and set by the curb with the rest of the garbage. I closed my eyes and floated, only vaguely aware of the front door opening and closing.

Concerned about my precarious mental state, Polly had come home between classes to check on me. When she found me unconscious, she crawled under the table screaming and shook me until I opened my eyes. I choked to her blurred image, in slurred sobs, that I had to die, that it hurt SO MUCH, that I could actually *feel* my brain and it was SORE and SURELY my nervous system would give out soon if she would just go away and let me stay there very still and very quiet. I told her I'd make sure to die with minimal noise and mess.

She said, "If you're going to die, don't you want to say good-bye to anyone? Surely you can stay alive long enough to do that. There must be someone." I told her I wanted to see Burke.

In an act I will always view as one of the most selfless anyone has ever bestowed upon me, Polly drove me to Burke's house. Maybe she called beforehand, maybe not. Maybe they lifted me into and out of the car. I do not remember walking. I wanted to be mothered, because my own mother would not do so. She was one of the people who thought I was behaving badly out of a need for attention, and we could no longer have a conversation without screaming. I lay my head on Burke's lap in his dark, wood-paneled living room, pretending I didn't know what I knew about him and Polly.

He was remarkably gentle. His hands were cool washcloths and Vicks VapoRub; his voice chicken soup and game shows. He wrapped me in a blanket and held me on the couch. I felt it was more than any doctor or hospital would do for me. Nonetheless, a hospital was exactly what he had in mind, and as I lay there apologizing and slipping in and out of sleep, Polly made the call.

They took me to Charter Vista, a private rehab hospital, the only place in town resembling a psych ward. I was the only patient who was not there to detox from alcohol or drugs. Charter was a veritable day spa compared to the hospitals I would see later, where incontinent schizophrenics flung wet diapers down the hallway and orderlies threatened shots of tranquilizers to make us behave, but it wasn't equipped to handle a wailing, dissociating borderline under the influence of nothing stronger than coffee, sugar, and weeks of insomnia. Still, they were able to give me a paper cup of Navane, a powerful antipsychotic, and I spent the next eighteen hours passed out cold.

I came to and hit the ground running. I smoked up a storm, chatted up the addicts, bummed cigarettes, and elaborated upon the great novelty of the lighter embedded in the wall. *I can still stick my hand in there,* I said. *I can still burn myself. I can still do damage.* That afternoon, my hospital-issue shrink said to me, "Look, there is some belief around here that you're manic." This was fine with me. Being manic was way better than being borderline, which meant you were hopeless and incurable. I happily accepted manic. Years later, upon getting the records from that hospitalization, I saw that their diagnoses went like this: Axis I, Mood Disorders: Manic Depression. Axis II, Personality Disorders: Borderline. These words are written in the files of every psychiatrist I have seen since.

Here's where the drugs come in. At Charter they commenced the fucking-with of the body chemistry, the advent of brown bottles and side effects. I stood on the edge of the diving board and the pool into which I would leap opened beneath

me and its name was—deep breath—Ritalin. After a few days
on Navane, I asked about the paradoxical effects of stimulants.
In 1993, attention deficit disorder had just become a trendy
diagnosis, so ADD drugs were fashionable as well. It was all
over the news how stimulants could calm you down. They told
me I could try it and know in an hour if it worked. I felt wired,
but convinced myself I felt calm, in large part because I also
knew that Ritalin caused weight loss. So I told my doctor I
liked it, and he wrote me a prescription. This is how I, the
manic girl, came to be given the drug whose generic name
starts with *m-e-t-h*.

Because I had no health insurance, I couldn't stay at Charter. After the seventy-two-hour waiting period was up, they
kept me one more day for good measure, and then dismissed
me and I was free to move to Cincinnati. Three days after that,
armed with a fresh theater degree and a bottle of stimulants,
I did.

ON THE WAY to Cincinnati I hung my left arm, and occasionally my head, out the car window. I screamed Ramones lyrics into cornfields and I talked back to the late-night wackjob
preachers. At 5 a.m., just across the Kentucky state line, I
pulled over at a KOA Kampground and took a shower I had to
pay for with quarters.

When my allotted burst of cold water ran out, I realized I'd
forgotten to bring clothing or a towel. All I could do was run
for it, across a damp field in the early morning, back to my Pon-
tiac Sunbird with the overheating transmission, naked. Grass

stuck to my wet legs and feet. The cows mooing in the nearby
fields were not the same cows as the day before, and this made
me delirious with joy. I clamped my hand over my mouth to
keep from laughing out loud and waking the campers. Water
dripped from my breasts and my chin and the tangles of my
hair. Back at the car I watered one little spot of the ground,
changed it with my presence, while I dug in my backseat for
something to cover myself.

I had just attempted suicide in Arkansas, and now it was
four days later and I was standing naked in a field in Kentucky.
I had left in my wake teachers, friends, and parents who were
terrified for my safety. My mother, however, insisted it had all
just been a bit of melodrama, and my father had been on the
road driving his truck through the whole thing. I had slipped
away before he could get Wal-Mart to let him come home.

11

"HOW DID YOU *do your tattoo?" I asked my Uncle Junior.*

"With a needle and thread. And India ink. Y'all probably don't know what India ink is these days."

"A needle and thread?"

"Yeah, you would just wrap the needle in the thread, and then dip it down in the ink and poke little holes in yourself, and the ink would go into your skin."

"But then it goes away?" His was so faded it was barely visible beneath the hair on his knuckle.

"Mine went away. It's supposed to last forever."

As with so many borderline suicidal gestures, the breakdown dissipated as quickly as it came on. As soon as I hit Cincinnati, I was wildly blissed out again. When manic, as when stoned, everything struck me as profound, such as the fact that in Cincinnati there are bookstores that hide from you. The city is made of hills covered with Victorian houses in various states of splendor and disrepair, and, short of Barcelona, it was the most magical place I'd ever seen. In one of the big old houses, on top of a hill near the university, in the shadowy ghetto underside of which I lived, was a bookstore called Bookstore. Their books were halfheartedly shelved; some of them were simply stacked slapdash upon the lower bodies of naked mannequins: books with legs. The top halves of the mannequins took up space on the various threadbare love seats scattered throughout the place. There was an entire room of *plays*. The first time I stumbled into the place, I was greeted with a book about Mummenschanz, when I'd just been——no lie——walking down the street thinking about Mummenschanz. I was in speed-fueled lit-dork love.

I lived in a three-story house with six other twenty-three-year-old theater interns from all over the country, and the usual drama ensued, but my brain was stimulated, so for the first few months it was a euphoric time. At night, after rehearsals, the other interns and I walked from the Ensemble to Kaldi's Coffee House, had long conversations about Theater with a capital T, and bonded over excessive amounts of very strong coffee. I took to smoking clove cigarettes and wearing my reading glasses all the time, primarily because I wanted to impress a boy, Reese, the lighting designer, and George, his musician friend. They both had beards, and George actually carried around bongo drums. Reese was lanky and delicate, thoughtful and smart, with shaggy black hair and glasses. He was divine, and I quickly promoted him to the exalted position of Love of My Life (du jour). I'd know once and for all that I was sophisticated, I reasoned, if I could just score a boyfriend who looked like Trotsky. And score I did: before long, Reese and I were a couple, head over heels, making out on the lighting grid late at night after rehearsals.

I shrank due to Ritalin and caffeine, my weight dropping to 125 pounds, but I was happier than I'd ever been in my life. I was in love, and I was on medication, and even if it wasn't the right medication, it certainly pepped me up and made me chipper. So what if I got a little bit anorexic again? I got a little bit anorexic again.

Which was, of course, the beginning of the downfall. For a while, everything was suspended, new. Everything sparkled, radiated, shone. I stood in front of the candy machine in the basement of the theater one night, staring at the gummy, multicolored Chuckles, swooning over the particular beauty of the black ones. The whole world opened up to be appreciated, and I was grateful for the chance to appreciate it—I just thought I'd be even more capable of doing so if I had a better body.

I coupled the Ritalin with cigarettes, and dropped twenty pounds in the first three months I was there. The nicotine, amphetamine, and frequent, vigorous sex with Reese were all I needed; nutrition seemed unnecessary. My roommates, who had said upon meeting me what most people say—"You're so full of energy"—rapidly grew annoyed as that energy became irritability, a boundless hyperactivity punctuated by grouchiness and aggression. In the parlance of bipolar disorder, this is called an "agitated mania," or a "mixed state." If mania is uncomfortable but fun, mixed states are uncomfortable and no fun at all.

Cincinnati was where I learned that running away from your problems has a three-month statute of limitations, a lesson I have found repeatedly to be true. Three months is still a first impression—of a city, of other people, of yourself in that place. But there comes a point when you can no longer hide who you are, and the reactions of others become all too familiar: they are afraid of you, have grown tired of you, unable to put up with the bottomless pit of your need and despair. You become disillusioned with them for being unable to do so, and the good old borderline "splitting" comes into play: they are mean, you are bad, everything is one way or the other and you have no more options than you did in the place from which you ran. As the people in Cincinnati turned into the people in Arkansas—directors stopped casting me, roommates and colleagues started avoiding me—I waited for the ultimate bomb to drop. I counted the days, the minutes, the breaths, until Reese broke up with me.

Which, of course, he did. Fall turned to winter and my beautiful new city turned to ice. One night I sat on Reese's bed, naked, shivering, and he told me I was just too much of an actress for him.

"What?" I squeaked, as my vision narrowed to that pinprick that precedes impending doom, the one where you know everything is about to change and you are in the last remaining seconds of the reality to which you have become accustomed.

"You just . . . sometimes you're just too *intense*. Like you're always acting."

Of all the words in the world I hate, *intense* may very well be the one I hate the most. It is certainly the one which, when leveled at me, carries with it the shame of all the times I've heard it before, and embarrasses me like a small child who has just peed her pants.

I remember he said, "I'm sorry," which of course the person dumping you never really is, or at least not enough that they're willing to stay with you. I remember running out the door and sitting in the hallway crying. I remember my black eyeliner dripping on my white T-shirt and leaving little dots. I remember half of me falling away, and my surprise that there always seemed another half of me to do so. What percentage of my original self was I by that point? A quarter? An eighth? A sixteenth?

I fell apart with a whole new level of tragedy and drama. My room in our big old drafty house was right next to the living room, and I couldn't bear having people that close to me. I decided I didn't deserve windows—there was always some new thing I didn't deserve—so I moved into the basement. Cincinnati had a record snowfall that winter, more snow than I had ever experienced in my life, and the one small window I did have was always obscured by drifts. Fair enough, I deserved that too. I found the black hole inside me and lived there, and as a prelude to a decade-long battle with the mental health care system, it was strangely peaceful.

As the Ohio River valley froze to a silver January, I slowed like a fish trapped beneath a top sheet of ice, occasionally looking up toward a vague memory of the sun. I came straight home from the theater every evening at six o'clock, went straight to the basement, and crawled into bed. I had only a mattress separated from the concrete floor by a thin piece of industrial carpet, which, given my lifelong tendency to pack my living space with as much color and art as possible, was the most obvious indication that I had thoroughly given up. I narrowed my life to nothing but survival and sleep, becoming a very efficient creature. I no longer did things for pleasure, so I required no excess light or water. I did not read or soak in bubble baths—in fact, I washed myself simply by squatting in the bathtub in front of the faucet, not even putting the plug in the drain. Comfort was too much trouble, as was standing up in the shower. I needed little energy, and as such, little food. That winter I simply waited to disappear.

Lying sleepless for hours on end beneath a pile of blankets and discarded clothes—too exhausting to put them on hangers, to figure out if they were dirty or clean; once a week I shoved the whole mass into the washer and threw them back on the bed when they were dry—I pretended I was a prisoner, doing time in my own head. I remembered a story we'd read at Governor's School, Ursula Le Guin's *The Ones Who Walk Away from Omelas*, in which the happiness of a utopian city is dependent upon one forgotten child suffering in a basement, a sacrificial victim. I pretended I was performing a meritorious act, as opposed to simply giving in to depression without a fight. I longed for uninterrupted sleep, but it never came—I catnapped like a prisoner constantly afraid of sudden attack. In my dreams, Reese left me over and over again.

People with borderline personality disorder are notorious for self-destruction in the face of breakups. The worst thing we can imagine is being called out on our faults and subsequently abandoned—the pain of betrayal is so intense it can feel as if the person who left us has taken our heart and soul with them. Unlike those with clinical depression, who generally contemplate and commit suicide quietly, borderlines do it loudly, making sure everyone around us knows about it. In the midst of the chronic interpersonal catastrophes that punctuate our lives, we cannot imagine that things have ever been better or that they ever will be. We are either invincible or wholly worthless, and if we're worthless, we might as well die, even if just the day before we felt capable of changing the world. The loss of love negates everything good about us. Never mind that everyone else in the world has gone through at least one bad breakup; ours—our current one, never any of the ones before—is *the worst*. Nobody else has ever experienced such pain, and the only relief from that pain is punishment, swift and severe. So we cut, or burn, or starve, or purge, or write all over ourselves with Sharpies, or imprison ourselves in basements. One in ten of us die by our own hand, not all of us intentionally. Borderlines have a very high rate of accidental suicide; in the heat of the moment, we make grand attempts, hoping to be saved, but sometimes no one comes along to save us.

The problem with the savior complex is that eventually our saviors get very tired indeed. It is too much trouble to keep dragging us back from the ledge, and it's not their job anyway. In the end, we can only save ourselves, but generally need psychiatric help to do it. I lay in the dark for months, until I could bear it no more and opened up the phone book one morning in search of a shrink who would see me even though I had no health insurance. I found exactly one place in town that offered sliding-scale fees: Central Clinic, the outpatient mental health facility of the University of Cincinnati. On a dark frigid February afternoon, I left the theater and hauled myself there. Now I think there should have been some sort of fanfare as I walked through the smudged glass doors, into the waiting room with its battered orange plastic chairs, cracked floor tiles, and threadbare rug. There should have been trumpets to herald the start of battle, the advent of war. There should have been someone to hand me the official uniform as I checked in at the grubby front desk and gave them my last twenty bucks. But there wasn't, there was only a tired-looking woman with a mountain of paperwork on her desk, to which she added my intake forms. I sat down to wait for my next redeemer to call me into his chambers, watching the schizophrenics who had just received their Clozaril shots shuffle past.

My god, I thought, *maybe that's what they'll do to me.* It was just like in the movies: right down the hall, human beings sacrificed their personalities and dreams to the piss-colored syrup in the syringe of some Nurse Ratched, and now I sat among them, waiting.

My first psychiatrist at Central Clinic was one Dr. Shores, who wore short-sleeved shirts that came untucked and with whom I would develop something of an alliance before his residency was over and I was handed off to the next incoming clinician. At our first session, he ate canned peas straight from the can. "I'm sorry," he said, "I didn't have time for lunch." He was well-meaning, Dr. Shores, if absentminded, and although he didn't sit around with me and talk about books, he did hand across his desk my second psychotropic prescription: this time, lithium.

For the unfamiliar, lithium is a hard-core, no-joke, we're-not-fucking-around-here drug. I talked to Dr. Shores for all of fifteen minutes before he diagnosed me as bipolar and wrote the prescription. So I stopped at the clinic pharmacy on my way out, and traded them three bucks in change scraped from the bottom of my purse for a plain brown bottle in a plain brown bag. In the bottle, little white tablets, *three a day*, and then home to learn about the crippling hell of psych med side effects.

Four days later, I found myself crawling around on the floor for two hours, looking for my car keys. This in itself might sound a bit excessive, maybe a little extreme, but not completely outside the range of acceptable human behavior. I mean, if you had to go somewhere really really important, and you lost your keys, and you had no other choice, you might be reduced to crawling on the floor for two hours looking for them. I, however, spent two hours looking because I kept forgetting what I was doing. Every now and then I'd sort of lift off from the launching pad of my brain, get distracted by a piece of lint, spend ten minutes pondering the lint, and then spend thirty more seconds looking for the car keys before I noticed a shiny object and had to stare blankly at that for a while. I know it was two hours because I looked at my watch a lot, seeing as how my wrist was right there in front of my face. Every now and then I'd think, *Hmm, fifty-five minutes and I still haven't found those goddamn keys, interesting.* On lithium, time completely ceased to be relevant. I decided, in fact, that time was a quaint, archaic concept, an outdated philosophical construct specific to Homo sapiens, which everyone followed because everyone else did. Whatever. It didn't apply to me.

I also began to guzzle water, and I rapidly gained fifteen pounds. I was a zombie, but at least I wasn't depressed. My roommates stole glances at me as if they weren't really looking, and talked to me as if they weren't really trying to figure out why I was rapidly becoming a big fat tofu who perpetually took up half the couch. I didn't care. I let them talk, and I put up no resistance, and I didn't talk about my personal drama because there was none. There was only acquiescence, and I was fairly pleasant. Reese even slept with me again, telling me he'd noticed I didn't seem like as much of an actress lately and that my ass was really hot now that I'd gained a few pounds. I wrapped my legs around him, because I knew he liked it, and I thought if I could just please one person for one minute maybe I could at least be good for something. Maybe there might at least be something I could do.

Eventually, of course, I would go for more pills. I would go back to Central Clinic over and over again, every time I got depressed, every two or three months. Because the clinic was part of a teaching hospital, the shrinks were there on rotation. So they said, *Here, take this,* and it was always a different they, and it was always a different this.

———

Ritalin.
Lithium.
Stelazine.
Navane.
Pamelor.
Prozac.
Effexor.
Luvox.
Paxil.
Depakote.
Neurontin.
Propranolol.
Ativan.
Ambien.
Adderall.
Lamictal.
Wellbutrin.
Seroquel.
Serzone.
Zyprexa.
Lexapro.
Celexa.
Cymbalta.
Trazodone.

Twenty-four drugs the parade of doctors dispensed in an effort to fix me. Fifteen years it has taken to find the three that work. Countless side effects: weight up, down; sleep elusive or never-ending; blood draws every three months to make sure my liver hasn't stopped working. Yet with every rip of a page off a prescription pad, I have dared to hope for rescue. The chemicals swim in my system, their names run together like a song, and sometimes I lie in bed chanting these names in an effort to calm myself. I sing to myself in whispers, waiting, wondering how many mad scientists it took to create the liquid I still, hopefully, longingly, call my blood.

12

THE FIRST TATTOO *that really hurt would be for him, for Reese.*
It's an armband of atomic symbols, because we talked about sci-
ence so much. The little blue and orange atoms dance around my
left bicep—all the way around, because my friend Tom stopped
his halfway when the artist got to his underarm, and he told me
I wouldn't be able to take the pain.

I took it. Because I couldn't have Reese inside me, I tattooed
him on me. When I sat in that chair in Cincinnati and the artist
drilled into my skin, I said goodbye: goodbye my love, goodbye
my Reese, goodbye to the one I thought was finally going to stay.

In 1995, at the age of twenty-four, I married a man ten years
my senior. I met Glenn shortly after Reese dumped me and

dated him for less than a year before we tied the knot. When my internship at the Ensemble ended, I floundered for something to do with myself, and on a whim auditioned for the M.F.A. acting program at the University of Cincinnati College-Conservatory of Music. I was accepted, and it was there I realized how much I hated actors and that I would rather write the plays than be in them. So I wrote one, and Kirby, who had started a theater company, produced it. Glenn was cast in the role of—wait for it—the shrink. (Of course there was a shrink; as the adage goes, write what you know.) The first time I met him, he had a toy clown in the pocket of his lab coat, held spoons in his deep-set eyes, and carried a book by William S. Burroughs.

I thought, as I always think when I fall in love with someone new, that he was the most amazing person I'd ever met. However, in Glenn's case, it actually turned out to be true. Certainly nobody has ever made me laugh harder or so relentlessly stuck by me through my craziness, telling me frequently that he could see my worth even if I couldn't, petting my head and calling me "little one" when I cried. For the next six years he stayed with me, unconditionally, and refused to be scared off by the breakdowns and hospitalizations and hairpin turns of mood. He stayed with me when I pounded his chest with my fists in a rage, when I hated myself over it, when I stayed in bed all day in the dark because I couldn't forgive myself for hitting him. He loved me when I was a whirling, screaming, Tasmanian devil of destruction. He put up with the fact that I still loved Reese, which was, unfortunately, one of the reasons the marriage ended. But most of all, when I really needed it, he protected me from my parents.

To be fair, he was also protecting them from me. My mother
and I fought bitterly in those years, because we both needed
to be understood more than we needed to understand one
another. When I was in high school, about the time I decided
religion was a hoax, my parents became deeply involved with
the church, becoming more fervent than they'd ever been
before. About the time I stopped watching *The 700 Club*, my
parents began saying grace every time they ate something.
In an interesting turn of events, we went from me trying to
save their souls to them trying to save mine. More than that,
we both needed to be right. My mother felt strongly that my
crazies could be cured if I'd just turn them over to Jesus. I
answered, loudly, IF THIS COULD BE PRAYED AWAY I'D
BE WELL.

My dad claimed to have found solace in Christ, to have
learned by studying the Bible that what he thought was mental illness was really sin. Although he had taken antidepressants off and on for years, he felt biblical teachings had worked
better. I began to look at my father and try to find his real self
in there, to catch glimpses of it in his eyes—sometimes I'd get
a quick look at his fire, and then he'd be placid again. I said
to myself, *This cannot be,* but some would say I'm lacking in
faith.

The first time I took Glenn to meet my parents, we drove
the 850 miles to Prairie Grove in our rickety Toyota, and all
the way I alternated between excitement and terror. I was surprised by the homesickness I felt in Cincinnati, and couldn't
wait to smell the Ozark Mountain air and show Glenn where
I came from. However, I dreaded being preached at, and I was

worried about how to hide my new tattoo. I was very proud of it and anxious to get more, but I knew I had to hide it from my parents or they'd go nuts.

You see where this story is going: I didn't hide it, they went nuts. The first night of our visit ended with a melodramatic blowout in which I lay crying and drooling on the floor, wailing that they just didn't understand me, and my mother, also in tears, told Glenn to take me back to Cincinnati because she couldn't handle me.

Glenn was caught in the middle, not just that night but for years, trying to figure out which crazy Pershall was most sane. Right off the bat, he was the diplomat. Our relationship mutated from husband and wife to surrogate parent and sobbing suicidal blob. Sex quickly became nonexistent, but we carried on for six years as if everything was okay. On the surface, my life during that time was relatively normal, consisting of grad school, waitressing jobs, and a lot of moving around—much like many other people's twenties. But most people don't threaten to kill themselves more days than not, and most people don't require their friends to be on constant suicide watch. Most people do not have the psych emergency room on speed-dial.

I finished my master's degree not in theater but in a "new media" program at the UC College of Art. Fascinated by this newfangled Internet thing, I developed live online performances, and upon my graduation I accepted a teaching job in New York City. In 1999, on my twenty-eighth birthday, Glenn and I sat in a traffic jam on the Brooklyn Bridge, in an overheating U-Haul with two yowling cats in a carrier between us.

Glenn truly hates big cities, preferring to live where he can take his telescopes out at night and look at the stars in peace. As he bitched at length about light pollution, I knew it was the beginning of the end.

If I had ever lost my mind before, it was just a warm-up for this, the main event.

My job was in the art department of a CUNY school, teaching animation and maintaining the computer lab. One day, looking for a Macintosh manual in another professor's office, I found a *Yahoo! Internet Life* magazine featuring Ana Voog. A Minneapolis performance artist and pioneering "camgirl," Ana broadcast her life twenty-four hours a day on webcams scattered throughout her apartment. The magazine was pink, her hair was pink, her website was pink, I adored her.

I contacted her that night and told her I was starting a webcam site too—because, ramping up to a manic episode, I instantaneously was. I flew into a wild frenzy of productivity that horrified Glenn, who was understandably pissed that I'd decided not just to drag him against his will to New York, but to broadcast our lives to the world.

Within days, I was so manic it hurt. My teeth tasted like metal. I couldn't stop grinding them. My jaw always ached. I couldn't sleep. The furniture turned to liquid and music broke apart. I stared at the clock all night.

Without consulting Glenn, I maxed out my credit cards on two new Macintosh computers and four video cameras. Now that I had a Real Job, I had been besieged by credit card offers, and I accepted. It was horrifyingly, scandalously easy to spend $15,000. It was thrilling, in the way that flinging yourself off a bridge is thrilling. You laugh hysterically as you go down.

It was also, unfortunately, way too easy to get Internet Famous. I was among the first camgirls to broadcast images from our homes, twenty-four hours a day. Fascinated by the trivialities of daily life, ours and others', we spied on each other constantly. Nothing was off-limits: bathing, sex, masturbation, bong hits, cleaning the kitchen; we were the queens of the overshare, we showed it all. Riding the cultural wave, I made myself a chartreuse website with way too much Flash animation and a soundtrack (when it loaded) by Esquivel. I named it atomcam, after my atom tattoo.

You can call it art all you want, but the bottom line is you're doing it for attention. Camgirls were a melodramatic lot, with much comedy and tragedy in our chat rooms. The gig was perfect for those who needed constant affirmation, as we all had a cadre of lonely older men and fellow angst-ridden girls at the ready to tell us how wonderful we were. If we were having breakdowns at 3 a.m., all we had to do was walk over to the computer and log into our chat rooms. If we wanted reassurance of our beauty, all we had to do was get naked and dance around the living room. It was instant gratification on a global scale.

In 1999, there was no Facebook, no MySpace, no easy way of finding someone unless they created a personal website. When blogs came about, it was a revolution. Ana and I jumped headlong into LiveJournal. Unfortunately, I didn't think about the possibility that I was signing a pact with the devil, forever making public things I could never live down.

I gleefully threw my crazies at the Internet, and the Internet ate it right up.

Glenn, however, did not. We fought constantly. I broadcast the fights in soundless stills that refreshed every thirty seconds, or every ten if you paid my $19.95 monthly membership fee. But when I was invited to speak on a panel about webcams at the South by Southwest Conference in Austin, Texas, Glenn said he was proud of me and helped me pack up all the cameras to take along. When I opened my bags at the hotel, I discovered he'd covered them with stickers. Ladybugs, because that's what he called me. I cried, but only until I went to a party and took some Ecstasy.

The manic episode I'd sustained for the last several months began its descent into the worst depression of my life the night I tried E. The combination of Ecstasy and antidepressants bathes the brain in a witches' brew of neurotransmitters, and how a mentally ill person will react to the concoction is anybody's guess. But that night in Austin, it was great fun, and I ended up in a whirlpool bathtub wearing a bright orange wig, sharing a Tootsie Pop with another chick.

Of course there was a boy. The one handing out the Tootsie Pops and filming the bathtub shenanigans, as a matter of fact. Jeremy was from D.C. and had a skinny ass, a skinny tie, and thick-framed black glasses, and of course he kissed me, and of course I fell in love. Right then, right there, as was my way. The fact that I was also in love with the pillows, the walls, and the smoothness of the TV made it no less magical. Borderline girl on E with hot guy paying attention, go. Time's a-wastin'. I gave him my heart as we tumbled into bed.

I returned to Brooklyn three days later, hungover, disheveled, possessed of only the haziest of memories of having said something on some panel, and having done everything but actual sex with Jeremy. If you're on drugs and there's no penetration, you're not cheating, right? Ha ha. Glenn took one look at me and knew. I cried and said I wanted a divorce.

While Glenn searched for a new apartment, I used what was left of the credit card to charge plane tickets to D.C. every other weekend. Then I got another credit card with a $5,000 limit and I maxed it out on same. When I wasn't with Jeremy, I fell apart and hated myself for what I'd done to the best person I'd ever known. The webcam broadcast hours and hours of me huddled on the futon, staring at the wall. I cried, and camgirl-parody sites collected the images and made an animated .gif of me crying.

Around that time my boss discovered my LiveJournal, wherein I regularly called her a joyless bitch. The day she rightfully fired me, I scraped half-assedly at my wrists with a Swiss Army knife until it was time to catch my flight to D.C. I was dead already; I had killed myself and my husband, I had ripped our hearts out and devoured them. The only thing left to do was fuck and eat Ecstasy until I got up the courage to commit suicide for real.

But Jeremy, oh, Jeremy! What a divine diversion. Jeremy was into raves. He bought me a pair of raver pants, even though we were thirty. One weekend he took me to a rave and I, in a Red Bull–fueled mixed state, got pissed off at the bouncer, kicked a hole in the wall, and got us both thrown out of the venue forever.

It was one of his favorite places, where he and his friends went every weekend.

"You still love me, right?" I begged him, tugging at my multicolored hair extensions as he drove silently back to his apartment. "You love me? Right? You're not going to break up with me?"

"I'm not going to break up with you," he said, lying.

When he dropped me off at the airport I made him promise one more time, even though I had ripped up all his photo albums over breakfast because they contained pictures of his ex-girlfriend. Unsurprisingly, I arrived home to an email dumping me. I sat there among Glenn's packed boxes and made a noise somewhere between laughing and screaming at the top of my lungs.

Here is where my real memories mix with what I've been told.

13

THE TATTOO ARTIST *inflicts pain and I take it. With each breath I count to one again. Each inhale, each exhale, time passes in the smallest of pieces, and pieces still smaller of those.*

This is how you count a life. This is how you go through it. Each second of hurt is a second that's already passed, one you never have to go through again. I have counted in pieces that small, when walking from the bed to the fridge seemed an insurmountable goal. I have counted my breaths, my steps, my eye-blinks, my hiccups, the tiny pulse in my thumb. And when I started getting tattooed, two of the things I used to need were gone: to write on myself, and to find irrelevant things to count. A second of intense pain is the most profound thing you can live through. And another, and another, and another, and then you know what it is to feel, and to struggle through that feeling one small agonizing increment at a time, and if you know that, you know what it is to live with mental illness.

I know I went into the bathroom, took all the pills from the cabinet, filled a big cup of water, and sat down on the floor. I arranged the bottles around me: Depakote, Celexa, Wellbutrin, and Seroquel. Just for good measure, I took out everything else in the cabinet too: Advil, St. John's wort, valerian root, Viagra. I began to swallow them, one at a time, then by twos and threes, then by the handful. I knew that if I thought about it at all, if for one second I let myself look up at my cats, I wouldn't be able to finish. So I just kept gulping them down.

I remember that I emptied the Seroquel bottle first, and that it scared and thrilled me to see the pills disappear. *I'm really doing it,* I thought. *It's really going to work this time.* I shook the bottle to make sure they were really all gone. Then the Wellbutrin, which can in and of itself seriously fuck you up if you take too much. Thirty pills? Too much. Top it off with thirty Celexa and you just may end up seizing and puking and passing out with your face in the toilet, which I did, on the Internet, forever and ever amen.

The bathroom camera (of course there was one) recorded it all, sending out an update every thirty seconds, old faithful. A woman named Terri who was writing a book about the camgirl phenomenon just happened to check in. She immediately called 911 and hopped in a cab. The ambulance was already there when she arrived, the webcam having broadcast the medics breaking in.

They took me to Long Island College Hospital, where the ER doctors put a tube down my throat and pumped me full of activated charcoal to neutralize the drugs. Terri sat in the emergency room all night, beside me, watching helplessly as the twin rivers of black sludge flowed into my nostrils. She watched as I thrashed on the stretcher. She told me later that every few minutes my arms and legs shot straight up in the air and shook, like a struggling overturned turtle. Between seizures, I vomited ebony streams.

At some point they pulled the tube out and I sat up and screamed. It felt like someone was ripping my intestines out through my nose. Then I slipped again into the muddy cave of unconsciousness, where black velvet bats brushed their wings against the insides of my eyelids.

A dirty drop ceiling with its pinhole constellations was my first clue that I had, unfortunately, made it out alive. The wall opposite me was one big window, through which I could see the blurry nurses floating. Beyond their station was another room just like mine. The nurses were in the middle of a circle of windowed cells, so they could see everyone at once. I had landed in Foucault's Panopticon, and we prisoners were patients in the ICU.

Probably the worst thing about waking up in a hospital, especially a psych ward, is that it's the ugliest place on earth. Long Island College ICU is the standard against which all other ugly things should be judged.

I needed to pee more than I had ever needed to pee in my life. I looked for the bathroom off my room, the kind they had at Methodist and Charter. There was none. I looked across the hall to see if it was there. It wasn't.

And then I saw the shabby yellowed shower curtain hanging to my right. It seemed to be blocking off the corner of the room. I pulled it back, and there, folded up in the strangest modular configuration I have ever seen, tucked away under a sink, was a stainless-steel toilet.

I am not kidding when I say that you had to pull the whole toilet down and sit on it quick before it smacked your ass on its way back up. I held it down with my knee, which is no easy feat when you have an IV in your hand and electrodes on your chest. With my left hand I clung to the bundle of wires attached to my body. Somehow I managed to scooch my underwear down, and saw that they were black. It looked like a pen had exploded. And then I remembered: the charcoal. After they give you the charcoal, they give you a laxative.

There were bruises all over my legs. I had never seen bruises like that before: huge black-and-purple blotches with irises of yellow. I had a vague memory of having fallen with great force, and would later learn I'd knocked over my computer chair having seizures. My limbs throbbed. My face felt bruised and swollen too. The toilet seat whacked my hip on its way back up and I doubled over, wincing.

Here I was, the girl Jeremy had once thought he wanted. The girl he would have continued to want if this cursing, crying, black-shitting thing hadn't taken over. All I knew was that I had two choices: either call him right then and there, and convince him to take me back, or get myself the hell out of this horrible place and go home and kill myself correctly.

The only problem was, there wasn't a phone in my room, and so Plan A was going to be difficult to accomplish. I thought about it for a minute and then yanked off one of the electrodes that connected me to the EKG. The machine went into a beeping, nurse-alerting frenzy. A woman in blue scrubs came running.

"I need a phone," I said.

She brought me one. She went out to the nurses' station and came back right away with one of those plastic see-through eighties Princess phones, the kind with a long tangly cord and bright, primary-colored electronic guts. She plugged it in for me and told me she'd be back in five minutes to clean me up.

What the hell kind of phone is this? I thought. *What the hell kind of hospital has folding stainless-steel toilets and Max Headroom fucking phones?*

I called Jeremy at work.

"It's me," I whimpered. "I'm in the hospital."

"I know," he said. "It's all over the Internet."

The thought hadn't even occurred to me that it might be. Who cared about me and my stupid boy problems? Who gave a shit if I lived or died? All over the Internet? What?

"I love you," I said. "I'm sorry. I'm so sorry."

He was quiet while I sobbed. Finally he said, "I think it's best if you don't call me again."

"What happened?" I pleaded. "Why are you doing this to me? What did I do wrong?"

"I really can't talk about this right now," he said, annoyed,

the voice that loved me gone. I was only a gnat again, buzzing around his head. He had seen the Bad Dog, and because
he was a smart boy who lined up his shoes and paid his bills
and brought his lunch from home, he wanted nothing to do
with it.

"Please," I begged, "please, I'm fine. I'm fine. I'm going to
get out of here today and I'll come to D.C. to see you. We'll
work it all out. Everything is going to be fine."

"I don't want you to do that. I really have to go back to work.
I can't talk about this here."

"Can you talk about it later?"

"I don't think that's a very good idea."

"But——"

"Listen to me," he said. "I am never going to date you
again. I'm being called by everyfuckingbody——the *New York
Post*, Montel Williams, every goddamn blog, and I'm about to
lose my job. Please do not ever speak to me again."

I dropped the receiver and howled. Oh my god, it was everywhere. For the first time the gravity of what I had done sank
in: I had tried to kill myself on the Internet. I had made history I never wanted to make, and nothing would ever be the
same.

Glenn had dropped off some clothes from home: my favorite
cotton pants, a T-shirt, and clean underwear. I just wanted to
get dressed. I wanted to wear my own clothes, to no longer
have my ass hanging out. They had taken away the gray shorts
and Velvet Underground shirt I assumed I was still wearing
when I came in, and had dressed me in a horrible hospital
gown. I was freezing. I couldn't get the T-shirt around the IV,

but at least I could change my underwear and cover my legs. I had managed to pull my pants halfway on when the nurse came back to bathe me.

"That's against the rules," she said.

"To get *dressed*?"

"Don't get smart with me. You came here because you tried to kill yourself. You're not going to run off and try again."

I couldn't believe it. Here I had just been told I could never speak to Jeremy again and now I was being told that I couldn't put on my own pants.

"How the fuck am I going to run off with a fucking IV and a fucking heart monitor? I'm cold. I just want to PUT ON MY FUCKING CLOTHES."

"I tell you what, missy, you just better watch that mouth of yours."

I had had enough. I was too furious to cry. I took off my pants and threw them at her. "Fuck fuck fuck fuck fuck," I said. "Fuck you. Go fuck yourself. Fuckity fucking fuck."

The response of my crackerjack treatment team, their humane and soothing reaction to my mental distress, was not to listen to me or try to comfort me or even bring me an extra blanket. Instead, they got an armed guard to come and sit outside my room.

I stared at him. He stared at the wall.

"I'm not going to kill myself. I'm not going to run away. You can leave now, you know."

He didn't move, didn't speak, just continued to sit there. I stuck out my tongue at him.

"Hey! Hey you! Look at me. I'm wearing a hospital gown.

They won't even let me cover my own ass. Do you know what this feels like? Has your life ever been so shitty that you tried to kill yourself? Do you have any fucking idea whatsoever what it feels like to be stuck in a hospital and denied your own clothing and told you can't even get warm and to be guarded by a guy with a gun, just because you're fucking SAD?"

Of course there was no response. He didn't even look at me. To him I was just some wacko, someone he had been told was dangerous, someone he had been given permission to tackle and restrain and maybe even shoot if she so much as tried to get dressed.

"I know you hear me!" I screamed. "I know you know that I'm a human being! I know you know what it's like to feel sad! You have skin and blood and bones and DNA and a brain, or at least I'm assuming you have a brain—"

A nurse came running. "What's the problem here?" she said.

"I'm not trying to escape. I just want to wear my own clothes," I sobbed. "If you insist on saving my life, then treat what's wrong with me. Let me talk to somebody. Get a psychiatrist in here. If I were here because I had a heart attack, you'd have let me see a cardiologist by now. You'd have let me put my pants on. Please. Please call off the dogs and get someone who can help me to convince you that I JUST WANT TO GET FUCKING WARM."

"I'll try," she said. "I'll see what I can do for you." But she didn't tell the guard to go away. He was on suicide watch.

It all just seemed so pointless. Here they had insisted on saving my life, just so they could punish me for wanting to end it. Exhausted and in pain, I sank into bed and cried myself to sleep, knowing for a fact that this was it. Things could not possibly get worse.

Sometime later I woke again, my eyes so swollen it took a minute to force them open. There were three shapes standing at the foot of my bed.

My mother said, "Hi sleepyhead."

Things had just gotten worse.

She, my father, and my cousin Kendra had flown from Tulsa to JFK, checked into the airport Marriott, and taken a fifty-dollar cab ride to Brooklyn. Glenn had called them the day before to tell them what had happened. They had used up a large part of their savings to get same-day tickets to New York, to sit by my bed and wait to see if I lived or died.

Seeing them there was the absolute worst thing imaginable. The guilt was overwhelming. There I was, the biggest loser ever, at the lowest point of a life I had just tried to throw away. I was bruised and bloated and my bleached, fried hair was a puffy mess. I looked and felt like hell. The last thing I wanted to see was my teary-eyed mother and my gorgeous perfect cousin standing there trying to pretend like they weren't in the most horrifying place on earth.

"I'm so sorry," I said.

"Shhh," said Kendra, sitting at the foot of my bed and rubbing my leg. "How do you feel?"

Like hell. Like shit. "I'm fine."

They sat in the room and made awkward small talk while the bells and whistles of the ICU went off around us. The whole time, I tried to figure out how I was going to pay them back for the money they had wasted on plane tickets. Their awkward presence in my world was jarring, inappropriate, wrong. I had done something terrible to bring them through the mirror, and I was ashamed.

We were saved by the first psychiatrist I'd seen since I arrived. He came in with two students, younger than me, wearing crisp white coats and frightened smiles. If there is one thing I hate in the world, it's psychiatry students. Especially after a suicide attempt. They stand there in their khaki pants and blue oxford-cloth shirts, creases pressed into the sleeves of their coats. The men have fresh haircuts and the women have perfect highlights with no root growth. They all look like they grew up playing soccer, with private swimming lessons and bright green lawns and Jeep Cherokees for their sixteenth birthdays. They go to the gym. They have never been depressed in their lives.

The psychiatrist asked me if I wanted an Ativan.

"Hell yes."

"We want you to spend one more night in ICU before you go to psych," he said. "We need to make sure your heartbeat is okay."

"My heartbeat is fine. I'm fine. My family's here. I want to go home."

"I'm sorry. It's mandatory that you spend at least twenty-four hours in psych after a suicide attempt."

The amount of hell I could raise about this was limited by the presence of my mother. "Fine," I said, "but only twenty-four hours. After that I'll sign myself out against medical advice if I have to."

"If your family agrees to take responsibility for you, that won't be necessary."

"About that Ativan . . ." I said.

My family spoke to him in the hallway and signed papers on a clipboard while the nurse brought in a syringe and shot me up. Within minutes I was drowsy. She bustled about getting my things together and helping me into a wheelchair to take me to the psych ward. An elevator ride, a trip down a long white hallway, and two sets of metal doors swung shut and locked behind us. The nurse wheeled me down the hall, which was surprisingly empty, and into my room, which looked like my college dorm. The wooden beds were covered with nicks and had words carved into them, though with what they had been carved, I had no idea. Mine said *lucky*.

The nurse helped me into bed. I tried not to think about the reason it had a vinyl mattress. I pulled the sheets up to my chin and screwed my eyes shut. It was the last peaceful sleep I would have for months.

The next day, my parents were given permission to take me back to their hotel. I wanted to go home, but it had apparently been decided that that was a bad idea. I knew better than to push it.

The one time in my life I've ever been in a limo was that morning. They had called for a car service in Brooklyn, and when they said there would be four passengers, the car service sent a limousine. So I walked out of the hospital, into the dilapidated, razor-wire-enclosed parking lot, wearing my faded cotton pants and ratty green T-shirt, and stepped right into the limo like I was going to the prom.

"Are you hungry?" my mother asked.

Surprisingly enough, I was. I couldn't remember having eaten anything during my stay. I wasn't even sure how long I'd been there. When we got to the hotel, my dad helped me into bed, took off my shoes, handed me the room service menu, and told me to order anything I wanted.

He was walking on eggshells. They all were. The only other time my family had ever ordered room service was at Disney World when I was twelve. Then I had drunk fresh-squeezed orange juice from a crystal goblet. Now I struggled to suck a chocolate milkshake through a straw. I had bitten my tongue so hard I winced with pain, but I tried not to let my family see.

For two days we stayed in the hotel and all I managed to swallow and keep down were chocolate shakes and mozzarella sticks. In fact, that would be all I ate for the next two weeks. Once a day, sugar and grease, then back to a comatose sleep.

I showered, finally, unsupervised. I let it pummel me as I examined my bruises. As the hot mist pulled the flimsy fabric shower curtain in on me, as it enveloped my body like the big white ball in *The Prisoner,* I sweated and tried to cry. I wanted to release my anger and sorrow as I released the hospital from my pores. I wanted the water to beat it out of me. But my heart and soul and brain were locked down, shut off tight. Whatever I felt now was trapped in the oddly shaped spaces between my heartbeats. (They had taken me off Wellbutrin after the overdose and put me on Lexapro, which sped up my heart rate.)

Kendra and I shared a bed. Just as we had when we were little girls spending the night at each other's houses, only this time everything was different. Two marriages, two children, three hospitalizations, and millions of dollars separated us now. She drove a BMW; I rode the subway. She had three houses; I was a month behind on rent. She was thin and beautiful, and I . . . well, I was doughy and beaten, black and purple, an obvious casualty of the outside world. She had succeeded. I had failed spectacularly, a fallen meteor giving up and cooling after crashing into the earth. I snuggled against her. She pretended not to wake up.

Eventually I had to go back to my apartment. On the third morning, outpatient treatment secured, we checked out of the hotel, and I held my mother's hand in a death grip as our cab approached the shabby brownstone. I was so grateful she was taking me seriously, that she hadn't let me come back to this place without making sure I had immediate therapy scheduled. I had a feeling I knew what was waiting for me, but I figured it would just be a barrage of emails and phone messages, not the goddamn *New York Post* hanging out on the stoop. My upstairs neighbors, who knew what had happened, told me the reporters were harassing the other tenants for information about me every time they walked out the door. They had been there for two days.

There were three of them, and my mother led me past them, my head bowed like a criminal. Once we were inside, my dad called the police, but apparently the reporters were allowed to stand outside the building as long as they didn't knock on the door.

The answering machine was blinking like mad. Even though I was already in shock, I wanted to get it over with, so I took a deep breath and hit the button. Apparently, attempting suicide on the Internet was of some great interest to the public, at least according to Montel and Maury and the *Post* and every other news outlet with a penchant for schadenfreude. I deleted them all immediately.

The phone rang. It was the *Post* again.

"Get your reporters off my goddamn stoop," I said.

"All we want is a quote," said the man on the other end.

"Sometimes people do things they'd like to live down and they want their fucking privacy. You are not getting a quote from me," I shouted, and hung up.

In the paper the next day was a story. "Sometimes people do things they'd like to live down and they want their . . . privacy," said Pershall in an interview with the *Post*. They had also called Glenn and quoted him similarly. The reporters went away.

Parody websites, the kind that exist to make fun of other people, called me everything from crazy to "a tattooed trucker bitch," to someone who should stop taking up space but was too stupid to kill herself correctly. I went numb, except for the incredible shame, guilt, and horror at having done something melodramatic I could never live down.

I vowed that day that I would never, under any circumstances, attempt suicide again. I had to find something to save myself—specifically, something besides a man. I had to channel the energy I had expended on self-destruction, on crisis after crisis, into something positive. Enough women hated themselves already; the world didn't need one more.

I would make my skin a place in which I could live.

14

DENISE IS DRAWING *on me, carving the story of my life into my body. I have become so used to her tools that they live behind my eyes and in my nostrils and my eardrums. The room we work in has a smell, green soap and A+D ointment; the things she does to me require germicides and antiseptic. She is another mad scientist, another strange girl, she whips off her latex gloves long enough to slap a piece of Scotch tape on the hair that keeps falling in her face.*

I love her. I gave her my skin.

On September 10, 2001, in the last hours of normalcy in New York City, I got my first big, visible tattoo: across my chest, from armpit to armpit. I went to a convention on Long Island

with a friend, and a large man named Baba, from Los Angeles, inked a smiling cat over my sternum. I needed to shout
to the world that my heart could be broken but I'd paint over
it with vivid colors. I would live, despite all the guys who'd
dumped me and the fact that a humiliating picture from the
worst day of my life would forever be available on the Internet.
The next morning, when the planes hit and I blinked awake
and said goodbye to my beloved city as I knew it, my freshly
abraded chest was covered with Saran Wrap wet with plasma
and Vaseline. It seemed fitting to have a bandage covering my
heart.

One night I was with a tattooed sort-of boyfriend who
lived in Jersey City, on our way to spend the night at his
house, when we ran into his neighbor Denise de la Cerda
on the PATH train. She had worked on him, and her pieces
were my favorites among his tattoos. He introduced us, and
in that instant, indefinable way, we recognized each other
as kindred spirits. The next day I went to visit her tattoo
shop, decorated with Buddhist altars and Tibetan masks
brought back by her Nepalese husband. The photographs
of her tattoos hanging on the wall took my breath away.
I was entranced by her work, how she used white in a way
I'd never seen before, how she crammed so much detail into
one tattoo. I asked her to begin painting the story of my life
into my skin.

There was a time when I liked to pride myself on my pain
tolerance, but as the years have worn on, I have run out of
nonpainful bodily real estate. A session is no longer a full
piece but a little more work on the one in progress. It's ago-

nizingly slow, and agonizing in general, but I am healing myself, and what this means for my friends is that while they no longer have to listen to my endless litany of emotional torment, they have to listen to me bitch about my inner-elbow abrasions and pretend not to know me when, in public places, I pause to dab saliva on the blood seeping from the cracking scabs on my ankles. It's all a trade-off, really. I hope they can see it that way.

Denise has told me that people have actually fallen asleep in her tattoo chair because she's so light-handed and her machines are so awesome, which makes me feel like the world's biggest pussy, seeing as how I've been known to bite my fist as the Nepali holds me down by the ankle.

"I'm sorry," I tell her. "Fuck, I'm twitching like a motherfucker." My vocabulary narrows to approximately twenty words when I'm getting tattooed, and five of them are variants of *fuck*.

But we always laugh. She goes back to inflicting pain and I go back to taking it. With each breath I count to one again. Each inhale, each exhale, time passes in the smallest of pieces, and pieces still smaller of those.

Knowing I can survive this, and that I have found in Denise a friend who so respects and understands my need to modify my body that she has agreed to commit to me for a long time. When Denise agreed to tattoo me from head to toe, a process that would easily take at least a decade, she said to me, *I will not leave you.* She deemed me worthy of patience, collaboration, and hours upon hours of her time.

Denise refers to the pictures she paints on me as "the shit

you let me get away with," but to me these tattoos signify my liftoff. My parents are, unfortunately, very opposed to them, and my mother has cried over them more than once. This kills me, of course, but I have tried to explain that this is something I have to do to reclaim my body, to experience and survive physical pain that approximates the mental.

A tattoo machine (not gun!) is built around a DC coil like the inside of a doorbell. On one end is a hammer, on the other is a metal tube. Tattoo needles are entomology pins or small sewing machine needles soldered in a cluster to the end of a long metal bar with a loop at one end. The loop is attached to the hammer and the bar passed through the tube so that the needles just barely stick out the end of the tube. The needles are dipped into small cups of ink. When the machine is connected to electric current, vibrating needles pull the ink into the tube. By the same token, the hammer drives the needle repeatedly into the dermis, the layer of skin just above the fat. The tattoo artist holds the tube like a pen, the machine resting on the top of her hand. The needles poke holes in the skin, and the ink is deposited into those holes. When a tattoo heals, it scabs over like an abrasion, which means the process of getting the tattoo feels a bit like getting road rash, if the road were made of angry bees.

Obviously, Karen Pershall is never going to approve of my doing this to myself, and I have learned to live with that. Although we love each other and have a better relationship now than we've ever had, I remember when, at sixteen, I tried in vain to explain to her why the stories I wrote contained curse words. When, at nineteen, I played Agnes of God and I had to prepare her for the molestation flashback scene; when, at thirty, I admitted to her I had been broadcasting my life on the Internet. Between being an artist and a mental patient, I have forced my mother to accept things no parent wants to know or see. But acceptance doesn't mean approval, and although my mother will now speak openly with me about my mental illness, she cuts to monosyllables when I mention my tattoos. The conversation goes something like this:

Me: I really should get off the phone now. I have to be
    somewhere at six.
Mom: Oh, where are you going?
Me: Denise's.
Mom: (*She knows who Denise is, thus she knows what
    this means.*) Well.
Me: Yeah, she's doing some work on my arm.
Mom: Well.
Me: So, yeah, I guess I should go. I love you.
Mom: Well.

She says it like this: *WaaAAAYYYYYulll.* It's two syllables. You draw the first one out, it gets longer and louder, and the *l*'s slam it shut. It's the verbal equivalent of smiling through your teeth and closing the door a little too hard on your way out.

What she doesn't say is, *When I see you now I think about your baby skin, how you were born on Mother's Day with jaundice, and how the doctors made me leave the hospital without you. I'm trying not to tell you what you looked like, yellow under those fluorescent lights with patches on your eyes. I'm trying to let you walk away now, trying to see the real you through your colors. I'm trying not to remember how when you were finally pink they let me take you home.*

Epilogue

PHILIP THORNTON IS *an old man now. He has white hair and age spots, but his smile is the same, and his glasses are the same: lenses without frames, gold wires that wrap around his ears. I sit on the edge of his leather chair and wonder whether or not to take my entire shirt off when I show him the tattoo.*

"I have something for you," I say.

"Is it a book?" he asks.

"No," I say. "Remember the last time we talked and I told you I was getting tattooed, and you said, 'Get a tattoo for me'?"

His head snaps back a little. He looks at me sideways. I turn my back to him, lift up my shirt.

"Oh my god," he shouts, and then he laughs and laughs. "Wildcat Frenchie."

Wildcat Frenchie was a burlesque girl in New Orleans in the 1950s. Phil, a student at Tulane, had a crush on her. To illustrate a point in one of our sessions many years ago, he'd told me about her. I delighted in teasing him about it.

Denise's rendition of her takes up my entire back. She stands on a pedestal. She has a black cat and a crystal ball, and her name is emblazoned six inches high and surrounded by peacock feathers. Over her head is a banner that reads Harm's Way.

"Do you remember?" I ask him. "Do you remember when you told me my job was to put myself in harm's way?"

"Oh, I remember." He lifts his glasses, wipes his eyes, shakes his head. "You always did take things a little too seriously."

What finally happened to drive me into dialectical behavioral therapy was one last bad relationship—this time with an author we'll call Shitnugget—in the spring of 2003. Although I had vowed never to attempt suicide again, Shitnugget drove me pretty close to it. I called my shrink, she sent an ambulance, and I ended up in the Bellevue emergency room. But wait, there's more: a month later I spent a night in jail for defacing copies of Shitnugget's book, with its front-page dedication to his penis, at a nearby Barnes & Noble. I ripped the covers off them the day they came out in paperback and hid them in the yoga and pilates section. As I was walking out of the store, a plainclothes security guard grabbed my bag and pulled me into the back room, where three managers, the eldest of whom was at least a decade younger than me, took their time in calling the cops. I was led in handcuffs through the store and taken to Central Booking, where crackheads threw water on me for being (a) white and (b) in jail for tearing up books.

I found myself once again letting my world shatter around me over a man, and I was mortified. How many times did I have to let it happen before I gave it up once and for all? Therapist after therapist heard how I couldn't live without the love of whatever schmuck had last crossed my field of vision. When someone, anyone, was mean to me, I still couldn't take it. I would melt in the floor of the deli sobbing and begging the forgiveness of the woman who called me a bitch when I bumped into her. I was exhausted from the effort of basic survival, and knew I had to stop everything and put all my energy into getting well before I killed myself or someone else.

All this is to say that tattoos alone didn't heal me, even though they went a long way. Once I started looking like an artist on the outside, I was much more comfortable being one on the inside. It was immediate and honest, and it felt good to have everything out in the open. However, medical and therapeutic intervention was still necessary.

Here is how the psych med story tends to go. After either (a) much convincing or (b) no convincing at all, we crazies march ourselves into the pharmacy one day with a fresh prescription for potential sanity. Once there, we may or may not fork over hundreds of dollars for a month's supply of pink or orange or yellow pills. If we're one of the lucky ones with health insurance, they hand over the bottle for little or no money, bestowing upon us a chance at getting better. If we're among the 46 million uninsured, well, tough shit, we'll just have to be depressed (or suicidal, or homicidal, as the case may be). Hav-

ing been uninsured for most of my adult life, I will always
remember the day when, at age thirty-five, I first handed my
new insurance card across the counter at Walgreen's and paid
three dollars for a thirty-day supply of a drug that normally
cost four hundred. I felt privileged, as if I had gained access
to some exclusive club, then felt guilty for feeling privileged,
then felt an overwhelming sense of relief, like for the first time
in my life I could take a breath that went all the way to the
bottom of my lungs. I found myself daydreaming about other
doctors I could visit: the orthopedist, the audiologist, the gyne-
cologist. Visions of annual pap smears danced in my head.

While we wait for the pills to take effect, we either (a)
worry about or (b) look forward to our new personality. Will
we recognize ourselves? We hope so, we hope not. In the ideal
situation, we will be ourselves, but enhanced—calmer, fun-
nier, the kind of person who could be described as stable. We
hope against hope that once the pills help us stop sabotaging
our relationships, pushing away and/or stalking our lovers,
and throwing things at people, maybe we'll get boyfriends or
girlfriends who stick around. We'll sleep better, wake without
dread, and our smiles will come back. We won't go on any
more impulsive shopping sprees, and we'll always be able to
pay our rent.

Or maybe we don't dare hope for a good life, because a good
life is a foreign concept. We wouldn't know it if it bit us. Instead,
we just hope for tranquillity, and if that comes at the expense
of having no personality and taking up permanent residence
on the couch, so be it. This was my experience on lithium, and
although it made me fat and boring, it allowed me to sleep.

One cannot overestimate the importance of sleep to the manic. However, I certainly wouldn't call lithium a success.

Psychiatrists, who these days tend to prescribe meds but not provide talk therapy, generally require a referral from a therapist, because them's the rules set forth by the managed care companies. This means we patients have to build trusting relationships with two doctors at once, show up for two sets of appointments, and repeat ourselves a lot. These are the hoops through which we must jump to get the drugs, to have our shot at Better. Because psychiatrists have ten more patients waiting in the lobby and need you to repeat yourself in shorthand, they love to assign scales to things. We are asked to describe our feelings on scales of 1 to 10: Are we depressed? Manic? Happy? Sad? Thinking of hurting ourselves or anyone else? Are things more or less hopeless than last week? Last month? Three minutes ago? We describe ourselves: Today I am a 5 of depression, a 6 of anxiety, a 2 of suicidal. I have often thought we should decide our numbers beforehand, and instead of reading old issues of *Golf Digest* in the waiting room, make labels to wear on our clothes. They can identify us by our numbers like inmates, if only for that day, and we won't have to say anything at all.

The question is, of course, at what numbers can we consider a drug successful? If I lower my depression score by 3 and raise my happy scale by 2, am I well? Do you have to be a certain universal number to qualify as sane, or is it relative based on how crazy you were to start with? Is my 6 of happiness somebody else's 8? If you're a 4 of happy on one drug but a 5 using another with more side effects, is that extra point worth gaining forty pounds (or twitching, or getting a rash, or experiencing involuntary movements of the tongue, or any of those other things they say veryveryfast at the end of drug commercials)?

I think of the whirlwind of side effects I've experienced, and it exhausts me. The massive lithium/Depakote/Seroquel weight gain, the shitting of my pants on Wellbutrin, the crippling dizziness that hits after 24.5 hours without Effexor. It should not be that if you take a pill at noon one day and twelve-thirty the next, your brain should come loose and send loud buzzing echoes ricocheting through your skull, but that is in fact what happens. Taking these medications requires vigilance, and if you are careless, there are serious consequences. It only takes one weekend of going out of town and leaving your meds at home to make you never, ever do it again. Once, deprived of Paxil for 48 hours, I spent a gruesome Sunday lying in a fetal position in a hotel room in Austin while my friends partied it up at South by Southwest. My day consisted of attempting to stand up and falling down because I was too dizzy, punctuated by unsuccessful attempts to drink orange juice with the tiniest of swallows, so as to induce only the smallest of brain shivers. A gulp left me clutching my head, pressing my fists into my eyeballs to stop the jolts.

I endured fifteen years of side effects and questionable efficacy before I was given Lamictal, the mood stabilizer that has, along with completing the full eighteen-month, three-day-a-week course of DBT, kept me out of the hospital for four years now. I greatly enjoy living a life not punctuated by suicide attempts, and I'm grateful to GlaxoSmithKline for their help. One thing that pisses me off royally is hearing drug companies denounced as the devil. I don't like giant corporations (or, in the words of Spalding Gray, "the big indifferent machine") any more than anyone else, but I *really* don't like wanting to kill myself. A person who denounces psychopharmaceuticals based on a political agenda is a person who has never lain crumpled in a ball in the closet, sobbing uncontrollably, face covered in Sharpie, throat raw from induced vomiting. Accordingly, that person should be thankful and shut the hell up.

While it is true that a drug which relieves symptoms in one person may exacerbate them in another, and that doctors thus have no way of knowing how a patient will respond to a drug unless they try it, misdiagnosis—and thus mismedication—is all too frequent. I would not have taken twenty-four drugs if I'd been diagnosed borderline in the first place. When I began to request my charts from the many clinics and hospitals where I've been treated, I was amazed that for the first ten years I sought help, shrink upon shrink diagnosed me bipolar and borderline, but none of them ever told me about the borderline part, the all-important Axis II. When a person is diagnosed with a mental illness, according to the DSM, she is given both an Axis I and Axis II diagnosis. Axis I comprises all conditions *except* personality disorders and mental retardation. This creates two major complications right off the bat. First, the Axis I disorder is seen as the primary illness in need of treatment, when in fact the personality disorder may be more prominent and troubling, and second, the Axis II diagnosis is much more open to interpretation, and therefore much harder to pin down. According to the DSM, "general diagnostic criteria [for an Axis II disorder] is an enduring pattern of inner experience and behavior that deviates markedly from the expectations of the individual's culture." Given the difficult task of defining that experience, it is no wonder misdiagnosis is rampant. Even though I'm a hell of a lot better than when I was first diagnosed, I daresay I continue to deviate from the expectations of my culture. But the journey of that deviance, the covering of my body in tattoos, has allowed me to make a tentative peace with my flesh. It has taught me that I am brave and can withstand tremendous pain. Not all deviance is negative; without it, we'd never change the world.

Still, I spent a lot of time wondering if I'd have been less borderline if I'd been raised by liberal artists in New York City. In Prairie Grove, if you don't bow your head and pray to Jesus, you're culturally transgressive. In New York, I have yet to hear anyone say grace before every meal, but my parents pray before eating a McDonald's cheeseburger. So am I only borderline according to Arkansas standards? The answer is *of course not*. I tried moving to Cincinnati, and after that Boston, and after that New York, and my illness followed me everywhere I went. There are very real and pervasive indicators of borderline personality disorder, particularly recurrent difficulty sustaining meaningful relationships. There was no question that this difficulty was central to my life and my sorrow.

This is where teasing out the entanglement of borderline and bipolar becomes crucial. Had an astute clinician had more than seventy-two hours to do this detangling during my first hospitalization, it would have saved me a lot of misdiagnoses, and thus reduced the number of ineffective medications whose side effects I suffered. (I do not think Phil Thornton misdiagnosed me; I think he was correct to treat the primary illness with which I presented: the eating disorder.) But more than that, it might have led to more efficient therapy, and greatly reduced the amount of money I spent on medication that didn't help, therapy that didn't help, and repeated hospitalization. It would also have reduced the amount paid by my insurance, on the all-too-fleeting occasions when I had insurance.

The back-asswards way in which this is viewed by insurance companies is as follows: Axis II disorders are long-term and acute. As such, many borderlines, including myself, suffer in silence for years before getting treatment simply because it is more cost-effective to treat only the Axis I disorder. Insurance providers read "long-term" as analogous to "too costly," and that's as far as it goes. This is why residential eating disorder treatment, for example, is largely ineffective. Although anorexia and bulimia are Axis I diagnoses, both are highly comorbid with a diagnosis of borderline (particularly bulimia). Because poor impulse control is one of the major difficulties borderlines face, and gorging and purging are nothing if not poor impulse control, it doesn't take a genius to see that if the personality disorder is not treated, the eating disorder can't be eradicated in thirty days or less. And we are lucky if even thirty days are covered.

The entire time I was in treatment at Central Clinic in Cincinnati, I was told I was bipolar. The clinicians there were caring but overwhelmed, interns just beginning to see individual patients, and inexperienced in the recognition of personality vs. mood disorders. If someone (say, me) comes in hyperactive and talking a mile a minute one day and suicidally depressed the next, it could be rapid-cycling bipolar disorder, or it could be a borderline reaction to circumstance. If, for example, I am dumped one day, I am desolate and the world seems hopeless, because I'm at the black end of the black-and-white thinking. If, the next day, the guy calls me up and says he'll still have sex with me, I shoot to the white end; the world is full of love and light. Everything is fine, I don't need to hurt myself, and I *certainly* don't need therapy.

Another complication: there are drugs definitively proven to help the bipolar, but not so the borderline. The most promising treatment for borderlines remains behavioral therapy—specifically, DBT—in which skills training provides us with the cognitive tools to manage our symptoms. Mood stabilizers have worked wonders for me, which has led more than one psychiatrist to affirm the bipolar diagnosis. The prevailing logic about BPD has, for some time, been that the disorder does not respond consistently to medication, and as such a borderline who responds to medication must have a comorbid Axis I disorder. However, a paper recently published by the National Alliance for Research on Schizophrenia and Depression (NARSAD) refutes this logic, stating:

> Many doctors think that BPD is a disorder that should be placed on the spectrum of impulse control disorders. Impulse control disorders include conditions like Antisocial Personality Disorder, Intermittent Explosive Disorder, and Pathological Gambling. Researchers have found that the impulsive nature of patients with these disor-

ders . . . predisposes the patient to aggressive and suicidal behaviors under duress . . . Biological studies show
inadequate regulation of serotonin, dopamine, and other
neurotransmitters in patients with BPD. Monoamine oxi-
dase (MAO) inhibitors, which prevent the breakdown of
norepinephrine and other neurotransmitters, appear to
be moderately helpful for patients experiencing rejection-
sensitive dysphoria (excessive sensitivity to real or imagined rejection).

So there is some evidence that borderlines respond to psych
meds. The problem is that none of this has been proven for
sure. For so long, BPD was seen as a "garbage can" diagnosis, a name—for lack of a better one—for the patients who
showed up frequently in emergency rooms and therapists'
offices, chronically threatening suicide in response to the normal vicissitudes of life. That borderlines failed to respond to
traditional psychoanalysis, to the degree that Freudian therapists spoke of our "coming apart on the couch," was further
"proof" of our hopelessness.

And so we floundered, until behavioral therapy came along.
For the first time, therapists saw positive response. However,
given our unresponsiveness to traditional talk therapy and our
tendency to drop out of treatment, due to factors such as ban-
ishing our therapists for perceived slights and failing to show
up for therapy on days when we were consumed by our own
personal dramas, cognitive behavioral therapy was only somewhat effective.

DBT changed all that, at least for me, because of two
things: the focus on the dialectic, or gray area, between good
and bad, and the strict adherence to the rules required. One
of the things you hear over and over again in DBT is that as
long as you haven't been hit by a piano, you're able to get yourself to therapy. Many times I've heard those in DBT say, "I
just couldn't get here," and therapists respond, "No, you didn't
want to." DBT therapists love to talk about "mood-dependent
behavior," and tell us frequently that we have the power to
"act opposite" to those moods. At first, we fight: *No, you don't
understand, he broke up with me, she called me a bitch, I failed
(a test, a job, a relationship, a person), I was paralyzed.* The DBT
response: *Could you still move your arms and legs? Then you
weren't paralyzed.*

This is, of course, infuriating, and our response to being
infuriated is to thrash and wail and rend our garments. When
we do this, our therapists sit quietly and wait for us to stop.
And eventually, seeing that we're not getting a response, we do
stop. This ability to stop is nothing short of miraculous to us,
and before long we see that, given a choice, feeling good is way
preferable to feeling shitty. The outbursts get less frequent,
we learn to calm ourselves down (sometimes, then most of the
time), and even if we relapse and lose our shit completely, our
therapists stick with us. Unless we hurt someone else or fail
to show up, we can't get kicked out of treatment (my program
at Payne Whitney had a very strict three-strikes-you're-out
policy, and if you were more than seven minutes late, that was
a strike. Seven minutes and thirty seconds and they wouldn't
let you in the door, period). But as long as we showed up, of

which we were, surprise of surprises, capable, our therapists wouldn't leave us. They would refuse to see us for twenty-four hours after a suicide attempt, teaching us that suicide attempts had consequences, but they would never refuse to see us simply for being difficult. They expected us to be difficult, and they didn't abandon us. That, for me, was the most astounding aspect of treatment, and the one for which I am most profoundly grateful.

DBT can change the lives of borderlines, particularly the concomitantly bipolar. I know that most people to whom the diagnostic criteria for borderline personality disorder apply are female. I enjoy pontificating about brain chemistry and pondering the whole chicken-and-egg question as it pertains to mental illness: Did I get this from my father's DNA or from his parenting? Did I get more of his neurotransmitters than my mother's and that's why we're so much alike? Or rather, is BPD a diagnosis that could be applied to just about any young, sensitive, artistic woman? I present to you the diagnostic criteria, and I set them forth with the corresponding suggestion that you could take almost any weird girl hiding in the art classroom on her lunch breaks, cleaning paintbrushes, listening to Cure CDs, and wearing too much black eyeliner, and you could run down this list and diagnose her as borderline.

But I remember the girl I was at sixteen, the one who had no idea who she was (*identity disturbance*) and who thought sometimes she existed and other times thought maybe she didn't (*unstable self-image*). Sometimes the only thing that seemed real was her self-righteous (*intense, perhaps inappropriate*)

anger, the acid fury she directed toward the willfully ignorant, those who refused to wonder and question and educate
themselves. When she thought she had found someone with
a similar level of passion, she fell in love easily and the fire
burned bright, but inevitably lovers disappointed her and she
wondered what she'd seen in them in the first place (*unstable
and intense interpersonal relationships, black-and-white thinking*). And I know I did the best thing I could for her when I got
her the hell out of Prairie Grove.

The most truthful assessment I can give of my mental
health at this time is that I struggle for it, and some days
it's relatively easy, and some days it's hard. The days when I
feel like I can conquer the world still alternate with the ones
where I lie in bed crying. It's just that now neither extreme is
quite as, well, extreme. The eating disorder is the hardest to
banish; I've lost way too many friendships, lovers, and oppor-
tunities over my hatred of my body and the evil things I've
done to it. Still, I don't know if I'll ever look in a mirror and
see what's really there. To anyone who thinks eating disorders
are something rich, bored white girls do to get attention, I
bid you bite me. I have frequent, intense, inappropriate outbursts of anger over the lies little girls are told about what is
beautiful.

I was the girl in whom most saw nothing and some saw
everything. There were just enough of the latter to keep me
alive. The Birkenstock-wearing vegetarian drama teachers, the manager at Sound Warehouse who introduced me to
weird bands and cult movies, my boss at the punk rock clothing store—these are the wolves who raised me. Every one of

them was, or is, some kind of outlaw. They taught me that the only thing that matters is *You, Speak*. The only thing we can do as human beings is tell our stories. In the end, that is the only power we ever had.

I will write this story on my body, anyone can read it, I will dance around the room.

Acknowledgments

It takes a posse to make a book. Here is mine:

Jill Bialosky, my editor at W. W. Norton, who plowed through a mountain of tangents and found the book at the center, and her astute assistants Adrienne Davich and Alison Liss, who are good at answering questions (and lots of them).

Penn Whaling, my agent, who took the risk, reminded me frequently to calm down, and could be counted on to whip out a rousing rendition of "Bohemian Rhapsody" when I needed it most.

Katie Boyle, Ann Rittenberg, Bonnie Egan, Marya Hornbacher, and Sydelle Kramer, who provided invaluable literary wisdom along the way.

Denise de la Cerda, Kathy Rosenfeld, Emma Feigenbaum,

Amy Stephenson, Scott Bateman, Nigel Melas, Jude Almeida, Todd Whitworth, Cera Byer, Alexandra and Catherine Chandler, Jean Vink, and Paul Bloch, my besties, who loved me through the years despite the crazies, and who could be counted on to read my countless drafts. You guys kick ass, seriously.

Butch, Karen, and Cameron Pershall, my amazing family, who instilled in me the bizarre Pershallian sense of humor and allowed me to use it to write a book. Thank you for always reading to me. I love you.

Sarah Johansson Locke, Sera Solstice, and the righteous babes of Alchemy Tribal Collective and Solstice Studio, who reminded me throughout the writing process that the most important thing, always, is to dance. *Lililililililili!*

William Faulkner and Flannery O'Connor, who, by singing to me, taught me everything I know about writing the music of Southern speech, and Anne Sexton, who provided the title.

The people of Prairie Grove, Arkansas, who have been overwhelmingly supportive and helpful.

And most of all, Glenn Becker, who knows the stories before I tell them and can retell them with sound effects. One day we will be cranky old tattooed people in rocking chairs on a porch, surrounded by cats, crabbing about how kids today can't spell. I love you most and best.